SUCCESS
MADE
SIMPLE

SUCCESS
MADE
SIMPLE

An Inside Look at Why
Amish Businesses Thrive

ERIK WESNER

Foreword by Donald B. Kraybill

 JOSSEY-BASS
A Wiley Imprint
www.josseybass.com

Published by Jossey-Bass
A Wiley Imprint
989 Market Street, San Francisco, CA 94103-1741—www.josseybass.com

Jossey-Bass books and products are available through most bookstores. To contact Jossey-Bass directly call our Customer Care Department within the U.S. at 800-956-7739, outside the U.S. at 317-572-3986, or fax 317-572-4002.

Jossey-Bass also publishes its books in a variety of electronic formats. Some content that appears in print may not be available in electronic books.

Library of Congress Cataloging-in-Publication Data

Wesner, Erik, 1978-
  Success made simple : an inside look at why Amish businesses thrive/Erik Wesner ; foreword by Donald B. Kraybill. – 1st ed.
    p. cm.
  Includes bibliographical references and index.
  ISBN 978-0-470-44237-1 (cloth)
  1. Success in business. 2. Amish–Social life and customs. I. Title.
  HF5386.W443 2010
  658.4'09–dc22
                                      2009048407
Printed in the United States of America
FIRST EDITION

HB Printing 10 9 8 7 6 5 4 3 2 1

For my parents,
Stan and Wanda

CONTENTS

FOREWORD

A surprising thing happened across America in recent years: many Amish farmers abandoned their plows to become entrepreneurs. And they succeeded. This quiet, mini Industrial Revolution in Amishland trailed the rise of factories in the larger society by more than a century.

Barefoot Amish entrepreneurs walked right out of cow stables to assume the ownership of microenterprises in dozens of communities. With no family lineage in business or cultural tradition in manufacturing, they founded hundreds of start-from-scratch operations. Today some nine thousand Amish-owned and -operated enterprises thrive in North America.

Most of these enterprises are *not* modest mom-and-pop operations selling homemade root beer, rugs, and brooms on back-road stands. Although many are small, and lean heavily on family labor, some have a dozen or more employees and annual sales above $5 million. Some shops manufacture products that are marketed across the nation, and occasionally even around the world. A few enterprises have contracts with businesses as diverse as Kmart and Ralph Lauren. Others craft upscale kitchens for homeowners in the suburbs of Chicago and New York City. Dozens of Amish entrepreneurs have regional and often national webs of dealers and retailers who distribute their products.

The rise of Amish enterprises was surprising because barefoot farmers were perhaps the most unlikely entrepreneurs, let alone successful ones. Moreover, it was remarkable because Amish "CEOs" faced not only the challenges of other small-business upstarts the world over but cultural hurdles as well within their communities.

The revolution was also striking because these novice entrepreneurs held only eighth-grade diplomas from one-room schools, not Ivy League MBAs. Moreover, most of them had the same teacher across all eight grades and, at best, several years of basic, pencil-computed arithmetic, minus even a handheld calculator. Missing from their credentials were courses in accounting, human resource management, systems analysis, and marketing. These homespun entrepreneurs started their businesses at ground zero without any of the textbook prerequisites for success.

The story is surprising for a third reason: Amish cultural taboos restrict many types of technology. Imagine trying to start a new business without tapping electricity from the public grid, installing a phone, or buying a computer—never mind a religious taboo on owning cars and trucks. Amish business owners face church regulations against advertising on radio and television and any ventures that would clash with their moral order. Selling cosmetics or televisions and transacting business on Sunday are unthinkable.

Entrepreneurs who accelerate too fast will receive visits from church leaders admonishing them about the sour effects of growth and the blowback from a large-scale operation that loads too much profit and power on the lap of the owner—a bad thing in egalitarian societies.

The most striking thing is this: Amish businesses succeed and flourish despite the cultural obstacles stacked atop the typical hurdles faced by business startups. As a scholar of Amish society, I've followed the rise of Amish entrepreneurs with great interest. In one study, my colleague Steven M. Nolt and I found that the failure rate of Amish enterprises was less than 5 percent over a five-year period. Such a low dropout rate is impressive on its own but dazzling when compared to a failure rate that soars above 65 percent for small-business starts in their first seven years in North America. The homespun Amish rate is even more astonishing considering that non-Amish entrepreneurs are plugging computers into the public grid, driving cars and trucks, and using computer-controlled manufacturing equipment.

To make the tale even more tantalizing, a few Amish owners have become serial entrepreneurs—growing a business and selling it off to outsiders, plunging the profits back into new startups, and then eventually selling off their second-generation business and searching for a new one. In other cases, owners will break a thriving business into two or three separate divisions and hand them over to their children.

How did barefoot farmers become such successful entrepreneurs and do it so quickly? What lessons can we learn from them? Erik Wesner addresses these basic questions in *Success Made Simple*. In dozens of face-to-face interviews with Amish business owners Wesner probes for answers to these intriguing questions about the secrets of Amish success. He parlays and distills their homemade recipes for productivity in ways that can benefit all entrepreneurs—from those beginning a business for the first time to old salts searching for ways to improve.

I know Wesner and his work well. I've accompanied him on interviews in Amish homes and businesses. He has an excellent grasp of Amish culture and a winsome way of making interviewees comfortable. It's no small feat to earn the trust and respect of people ensconced in a different culture, yet it's one that comes easily for Wesner. He has a gift for opening doors and digging deep to discover the reasons that propel Amish entrepreneurs toward success. Moreover, his creative writing style tells the story with clarity and even hilarity.

The story that emerges from *Success Made Simple* is filled with irony. For many Americans, the Amish, at first blush, appear as a backward people, out of step with the march of so-called progress, and shunning many gadgets of our high-tech society. Nevertheless, these people without worldly accoutrements or credentials have applied an uncanny savvy, a dose of common sense, an ethic of hard work, and a bushel of enduring values to the world of business, in turn sprouting profitable enterprises. And ironically, in this fascinating and well-told story, we well-credentialed "moderns" have much to learn from these down-to-earth folks.

Elizabethtown, Pennsylvania   Donald B. Kraybill
January 2010

———

Donald B. Kraybill is senior fellow in the Young Center for Anabaptist and Pietist Studies at Elizabethtown College (Pennsylvania), coauthor, with Steven M. Nolt, of *Amish Enterprise: From Plows to Profits*, and coauthor, with Steven M. Nolt and David L. Weaver-Zercher, of *Amish Grace: How Forgiveness Transcended Tragedy.*

Unearthing the Secrets

I pull my truck into the drive, unsure whether to continue. It's mid-afternoon, and I'm down on my numbers for the day, so I decide to press the gas. Riding down the long dirt lane toward the weathered farmhouse, it takes me a minute to register what's missing: power lines.

As I grab my sample case, I am unusually apprehensive. In my sixth season selling books for Nashville's Southwestern Company, I rarely flinch when approaching a prospect—from big brick homes manned by stare-you-down after-work dads to backwoods trailers, where you don't know whether to expect a handshake or the barrel of a Winchester. But somehow the unassuming head-scarved figure standing in the yard intimidates me in a way that others never have.

As I approach the housewife, I notice her two young girls, seated at the picnic table nearby, conversing in a language that's clearly not my own.

This sales call falls flat; I sell no books today. Later, I find out that Amish speak their own dialect at home and that Amish women rarely make large purchases without the counsel of their husbands—a few of many lessons I would learn doing business in Amish communities.

Some five years, twenty settlements, and five thousand Amish homes later, the Amish don't seem so odd anymore. In fact, in a wired America that opts for Amazon and online searches, they turned out to be ideal prospects. While the eighth-grade-educated Amish didn't respond to my college-prep materials, a follow-up with a Bible-oriented product proved a huge hit. In Amish communities from Illinois to Indiana to Pennsylvania, the Family Bible Library set rests on many bookshelves, a classic that is treasured and passed from one generation to the next.

Salespeople get a bad rap. Direct sellers, in particular, often find themselves stuck somewhere between trial lawyers and repo men in the public estimation. They're pushy, untrustworthy, sell suspect products, and usually don't take no for an answer.

At least that's the stereotype.

Working an eighty-hour week, visiting thirty-plus homes a day, enduring the doldrums of refusal in an entrepreneurial pressure cooker over an intense three months would be most people's idea of a miserable way to spend a summer. But in terms of raw business training, there is perhaps no better preparation in learning human nature, organization, and self-management, and in overcoming challenges. As the thousands of company alumni who've done the job successfully over the years can attest—including leading businesspeople, state governors, authors, doctors, and teachers, among others—it's an experience that can shape a person in important ways.

Doing business with Amish in communities from Kalona, Iowa, to Lancaster, Pennsylvania, I enjoyed a firsthand look into their own successful businesses. Many of my Amish customers signed the dotted line amid the din of a bustling furniture-making facility or leaning over the counter of an at-home retail shop. Later, studying the Amish as a research fellow at Lancaster County's Elizabethtown College, writing an Amish-themed blog, as well as living and working among them, I gained a deeper appreciation for Amish society. Though I quickly learned that Amish are as human as the rest of us, I came to admire them for the qualities that typically attract outsiders: their sense of simplicity and honesty, and their emphasis on community.

I often saw evidence of these traits in business dealings with Amish as well, which, as it turned out, gave a clue as to why Amish companies were flourishing. The ability of Amish people—many of whom are sharp and streetwise in a way that seems to belie the "in the world but not of the world" faith tenet—to succeed in the arena of business was also something I came to appreciate. After reading Donald Kraybill and Steven Nolt's *Amish Enterprise*—a sociological exploration of the Amish business phenomenon—I began to wonder if the Amish business story had something to offer the rest of us. It turns out it does.

Delving deeper into Amish entrepreneurship revealed a community thriving in ways not just linked to the bottom line. In research- ing this book, I focused on the two largest—and arguably most entrepreneurial—Amish settlements, in Holmes County, Ohio, and Lancaster County, Pennsylvania. I interviewed sixty Amish firm owners employing roughly four hundred employees, chosen from across the size and experience spectrum. They include contractors who have spent years building in up-and-down markets, accountants, wholesalers, a buggy builder, and custom furniture makers who create plush bedroom sets for wealthy suburbanites. Some are second-generation businesses, but most were started by the current owner. Most operate as sole proprietorships, often in direct competition with one another.

As Kraybill and Nolt explain, the societal shift from agriculture into small business has enabled Amish to maintain a plain lifestyle, support large families, and ultimately keep their children in the faith. In these and in other areas they've had resounding success.

But—as I learned the hard way—speaking with Amish about success is not always easy. I recall asking a nationally known Amish manufacturer to share a few "words of wisdom" on a management question. His terse reply: "I don't have any words of wisdom." Full stop. Only after a considerable pause, and further prodding and softening of the terminology, would he continue to offer his thoughts.

Sometimes, praising an Amishman's business skills can border on the offensive. Asked about success, the typical Amishman, accustomed to avoiding *gross feelich* ("big feeling"), will more likely point to external factors than to himself as the cause. Instinct says, "It's not me; it's something else"—God, employees, good fortune.

That said, Amish do recognize business success, though the definition of success itself can vary somewhat from the popular perception. Concepts such as personal advancement and a high-consumption lifestyle factor less prominently, if at all. Rather, Amish tend to keep in mind that business is first a means to realize core goals, ones which don't usually come right to mind when thinking "business prosperity."

When it comes to those goals, ambitions may vary from individual to individual, but certain aims repeat themselves. Family and preservation of lifestyle. Passing something of value on to the next generation. And, of course, the ultimate: getting everyone into heaven.

Amish business owners enjoy certain advantages as members of their communities. Among other things, they benefit from a quality Amish labor force, intrinsic market appeal to the non-Amish public, and community relationships that foster bonds of trust and help to reduce costs in areas such as hiring and firing.

At the same time, Amish business owners face numerous obstacles resulting from the cultural restrictions of their communities. These include constraints on the ownership and use of technology, which reduce efficiency and add expense; cultural taboos, which can hamstring product promotion to the non-Amish public; and, for the most part, a lack of legal protection, since Amish do not sue, at times leaving them exposed to unscrupulous outsiders.

Resources and restraints act against each other in the Amish business arena. Yet, in the end, it's the entrepreneurs themselves that make the vital difference in entrepreneurial success, and it's from them that we can learn lessons for businesses in any culture.

The voices contained in this book express Amish ideas on business success. And, like the Amish, I take the concept to mean more than just the bottom line. As Amish well understand, "business success" incorporates the financial aspect. Yet the idea goes further. I explore business success in the traditional monetary sense, while looking beyond the numbers to examine deeper meanings of the concept, and their relevance for modern business owners as well.

As I researched Amish business success, a few key concepts emerged. Foremost are two: Business is a vehicle for something more important. And, you can't do it all on your own. The tight-knit Amish realize that it takes strong relationships—forged with employees, customers, other companies, and other members of the community—to achieve success.

In the following pages, we'll examine how Amish hire, sell, create, learn, market, and manage, all while keeping these concepts in mind. The Amish voices you'll hear may sound quaint at times. In other cases they may sound like any neighbor.

One thing is certain, though. The principles these remarkable businesspeople illustrate, reflective of human nature and raw business realities, are universal enough to apply in any arena—whether you prefer "talking *Deitsch*" or just plain English.

January 2010   Erik Wesner
                                                        Raleigh, North Carolina

A NOTE ON NAMES

In deference to the importance Amish place on humility, all names have been changed. Identical last names are typical in Amish society, and the naming used in this book reflects that—although individuals with matching last names are not necessarily closely related. In a few cases, nonessential identifying details have been omitted.

Non-Amish people and businesses are referred to as "non-Amish," "modern," or "English," the last a term Amish typically use for their modern-world neighbors.

CHAPTER ONE

EYE TO THE HORIZON

Cultivating a Vision and Thriving Through Crisis

If you don't have a dream, what do you got?
—PENNSYLVANIA AMISH ENTREPRENEUR

The patchwork acres and stone barns of the Amish settlement in Lancaster County, Pennsylvania, seem to reflect a way of life from a time well past.

Eighteenth-century forefathers laid the agrarian foundation that has supported the Amish for nearly three centuries in North America. Amish dress, transportation, and aversion to worldly ways have changed but slowly and incrementally in the years since.

Until a few decades ago, the farming vocation was the primary way to make a living as an Amishman. Milk checks made few Amish rich, but that was never the point.

Farming was a means to raise a family in an environment mostly shielded from the urbane influence of the world. Farming also meant continuity. The tangible assets of fields and meadows—and a way of life based around tending the land—were passed from father to son for generations.

Across America today, Amish farmers continue to cultivate their fields. But the real story is what's been happening in the buildings and shops that have sprung up next to the barns.

Driven by necessity, the Amish have laid a new entrepreneurial economy atop their agrarian heritage, in the process becoming one of the most unexpected business success stories in recent memory.

Amish businesses provide for vibrant communities whose members exist in a way their modern-living neighbors would consider primitive. Yet the firms the Amish run are far from backward when it comes to satisfying customers. Some sell nationwide and overseas— multimillion-dollar operations are not unheard of—while creating employment in their rural corners of America.

The Amish business example, pivoting around concepts such as integrity, family, and simplicity, is rife with insight for application in the modern business environment. And in examining the Amish business story, a good place to start is with the motives and visions that drive these robust small companies.

Regardless of whether you put on pinstripes or suspenders in the morning, having a well-formulated vision is an indispensable part of business success. A guiding vision proves particularly relevant when the start is harder than expected, when recession strikes, or when a newcomer challenges a long-established market position.

Ups and downs alike present challenges to owners and managers. A guiding vision, undergirded by integrity and personal commitment, can keep spirits up and focus sharp in lean times, and feet grounded in good times. A clearly formulated and internalized vision safeguards integrity when ethical issues are on the line.

Just like the family dairy, the Amish-owned business has served as a vehicle to support large clans and to entrust trades. While the temptations of prosperity have proven problematic for some, the typical Amish business motive is anything but consumption-centered.

Amish forefathers sowed their acres with the ultimate aim of perpetuating family and faith. Amish entrepreneurs today cultivate their businesses with similar ambitions in mind. Along with this cultural ideal, however, comes the individual vision of each Amishman, which naturally varies, just as it differs among non-Amish.

In this chapter we'll examine business visions of successful Amish entrepreneurs, and how they serve to buttress business achievement. We'll also look at some Amish start-up stories and lessons learned along the way.

The start can prove particularly difficult, especially when initial enthusiasm sputters out in the face of discouraging results. We'll explore what it takes to persevere when faced with weak sales figures or when all you seem to hear are doomsayers.

We'll also ponder the role that faith plays in running a firm—an unsurprisingly prominent element in a God-centered culture. Finally, we'll examine what to consider when formulating a business vision, a topic we revisit in the final chapter.

Amish may seem different from the rest of us, but their motivations, challenges, and hang-ups are frequently the same. Ultimately, the entrepreneurial experience of the Amish shows that business issues commonly seen in the "real" world in fact transcend cultural bounds, and that the tools and strategies they rely on are present in the modern toolbox as well.

CULTIVATING A VISION

Scanning Amish-themed features in the media, one comes across a well-worn journalistic template. It's the portrayal of the Amish as a stand-offish, world-wary folk, suspicious of modernity and staunchly insular. Many pieces start with a standard assumption of the Amish as pious Luddites, wanting as little to do with us modern backsliders as possible. *"Get thee gone, Englishman,"* they seem to murmur between the lines.

True, the Amish *do* delineate their world from the non-Amish one, making important distinctions that help preserve the integrity of their faith and communities. But get to know enough Amish people, and the aloof and prickly portrayal starts to wear thin.

Case in point: Jonas Lapp. Jonas is a "people person" in every sense of the phrase. I recall first approaching his Pennsylvania home, unannounced, on a muggy July evening. Suddenly, the Amishman materialized, nearly throwing the door off its hinges. Before I could open my mouth, I found myself tractor-beamed into the house. *Have we met already?*

I'd hardly recited my name before Jonas, bright eyes and beaming smile, had me at the kitchen table in front of a couple slices of his wife's pizza. On my return visit a half-year later, Jonas's children frolicked, and a handmade mailbox sign announced a new baby boy to passersby.

The second time around, the veteran homebuilder was no less hospitable, sharing ideas on his trade and on business in general. The whole time Jonas hammered away at one concept: *relationships*. That came as no surprise, based on my experience with Jonas, and his Amish neighbors' warm comments about him.

Jonas relishes what he does. But you can see that it's less the actual construction of homes or the financial payoff that drive him. Instead, it's the chance to be a father figure to an employee who never had one, to form a friendship with a "customer" who in the end never even does business with him, to do his small part to strengthen ties in his community.

"Builder" is a hat Jonas wears, one that allows him to achieve higher-plane ends such as these. But it didn't always come so easy, nor provide so much satisfaction. Early on, Jonas struggled with the *F* word.

Fear.

"I got into business ... scared," he admits. "I knew there was a chance to make more money, a better opportunity." But, he says, "I probably believed a lot of lies about business."

Lies?

" 'It's tough.' 'You probably won't make it.' People talked about the ones that didn't make it—not about the ones that were doing well. And you kind of buy into that. So the first two to three years I was running the business scared.

"And that's aggressive," he concedes. "You get very aggressive when you have fear of not making it. But it's not healthy."

Fear poisons motivations. When operating anchored in fear, he explains, "you're not establishing relationships. You're in it for what you can grab today. You're after as much as you can get.

"You try to do a good job, but as fast as you can. And the relationship thing? Well, I don't know if I'm going to be in it long term.

"Because you have this thought in the back of your mind," Jonas continues, "that this might be the last year the economy's gonna be strong. This might be the last year before there's a recession. This might be the last year before I fall and break both legs and I can't do this again."

Talking to Jonas, you get the sense that he's been through his share of rough spots. Recounting start-up struggles, Jonas feels that early challenges are often rooted in a person's mentality more than anything else. And so having a solid grounding plays an important part.

And here's where the other *F* word comes in.

Jonas's *faith* is what grounds him. He returns to it over and over. "After a bit you start to look around, and you start to realize that God is long term. And the Lord's going to take care of you.

"And if you really believe he's gonna take care of you, then you should start doing business like God's going to take care of you."

Amish lean on faith. It's a seemingly bottomless source of strength and security. Faith helps them see hope when tragedy strikes. Faith fosters gratitude in the fortunate. It's a basic element of Amish life and, by extension, their approach to business.

Whatever grounds you—spirituality, family, core principles—what matters is being actively aware of it, and understanding its importance.

Mission statements have long fulfilled this "grounding" role, at least on a companywide level. Some firms take mission statements seriously. For others, they seem to serve more as wall decor or as marketing tools.

The idea of a mission statement does fit inside the concept of *vision*, but the two are not one and the same.

The concept of business vision can be somewhat difficult to pin down, but it typically includes a company's or business owner's more general goals: the needs it plans to fulfill, the unique qualities it aims to bring to the table, how large, how much, what, when, and where.

Yet *vision* also takes in the individual's perception of his own role in the business, and how the business is meant to intersect with everyday, "nonbusiness" life. Vision, by its very nature, motivates.

Vision can include the potential positive impacts a company desires to have on a community, a market, and in the most profound cases, the country or world. Creating a vision encourages imagining how life could be different for you as well as for others whom your business can possibly influence—your customers, employees, neighbors, and family.

Mission statements typically capture a company's aims and ambitions in a market context and often take into account some of the impacts just mentioned. But a personal business vision necessarily includes in its scope how running a company affects the owner and his immediate environment, as well as what he and others can be or *become* through the business activity. A well-formulated, deeply held vision is often highly personal.

HEAD CHECK

Vision can also be a crucial source of strength. Fear takes over when we focus on failure. Jonas's vision has helped him battle and destroy this disabling emotion.

Jonas neutralizes fear by shifting his focus. "If you're a servant-leader, that means other people are gonna come first," he explains. "People have to be very important to you. You're not in it for the dollar anymore . . . you're in it to help people. And the profits? They come.

"People need people that will take the time to make them [feel] important." He sees the people focus as part of a personal mission. In Jonas's vision, he is a mentor to his employees, an ear for his customers, a reliable partner for his business peers. He executes in the day-to-day, while the far-horizon focus frames each decision.

When we are oblivious to all other concerns but our own, minor issues take on far more importance than they deserve. Directing our concern outward and acting to aid our fellow man is one of the greatest fear-destroyers in the modern businessperson's arsenal. But to do this, you need both humility and an ability to empathize.

Jonas raises another worthy point relating to vision: sorting out motives and ambitions before techniques and strategies. Vision is concerned with the *why* before the *how*. It may have taken a journey to get there, but Jonas has his *why* sorted out—in his case, to be a person who adds value to others' experiences, be it by mentoring, listening, or collaborating as a contributing, productive member of his community.

Are you long term or day-to-day? While entrepreneurs like Jonas stress the importance of the here and now, at the same time they realize they must have a long-term vision to be effective in the day-to-day—in Jonas's case to avoid the place of fear by residing in concern for his fellow man.

Small-business owners can be providers in numerous meaningful ways: products or services that improve lives; jobs for members of the community; contributions to charitable causes. Amish bosses who provide these things often stress the good of others before they get to talking about their own pockets.

At the same time, successful Amish businesspeople take great satisfaction in the roles they create for themselves and in the fruits of their labors. The examples of Jonas and others seem to suggest one question relevant to anyone who is considering, or reevaluating, a personal business vision: *Where's your head?*

HEAD CHECK, PART 2

Getting your head right also means locking down the raw, nuts-and-bolts knowledge needed to achieve competence in your field. At the same time, mastering the tech side is only one slice of the pie. And in some cases, in a managerial context, intimate knowledge of every procedure in your firm not only is unnecessary but can even become an obstacle, leading overzealous managers to lose sight of the wide view.

In the business classic *The E-Myth Revisited*, Michael Gerber explores a basic error, which he terms the Fatal Assumption: Just because you are good at doing something means you're ready to make a business of it.

Like their English counterparts, Amish businesspeople often seek guidance at some point in their business lives. As we'll examine in the next chapter, this may take the form of offhand consulting with a father or brother or neighbor. It could mean seminars and books. It may even mean kicking ideas around with their current boss—some of whom are surprisingly supportive of their employees' entrepreneurial ambitions. The wiser entrepreneurs identify what they are lacking and supplement the missing bits. The Amish even have their own consultants.

Isaac Smoker is a deliberate man who weighs every comment carefully before speaking. Neighbors and fellow church members alike speak highly of him. Seen as an authority, Isaac is trusted for his no-nonsense business counsel. At the same time, Isaac, a bishop, fulfills a valuable function, guiding his business contemporaries and coreligionists on how to stay true to their beliefs and cultural practices while running successful firms in a non-Amish world.

A business owner himself, Isaac works with a number of Amish-run companies and is well positioned to observe the development of businesses among his people. Talking about typical mistakes, he says that one "problem is they go from working for someone else to forming their own company overnight." The main issue, Isaac points out, is that "maybe they're not really suited to be running a company; maybe they're not really suited for the business they're in.

"They think they know how to work, and they don't realize that running a business is something else." Ignoring the fact that business is about a lot more than just efficiently pumping out widgets is a common hazard for would-be company managers. Gerber writes in *E-Myth* that "when the technician falls prey to the Fatal Assumption, the business that was supposed to free him from the limitations of working for somebody else actually enslaves him."

According to Gerber, what happens is that "the job he knew how to do so well becomes one job he knows how to do plus a dozen others he doesn't know how to do at all."

Lancaster homebuilder Elam Peachey realizes this today.

"That was me," he confesses, describing a start-up experience matching Isaac's example. "I knew how to build the house, but I didn't . . . know anything about [the business side]. But I wasn't gonna let it stop me.

"The office thing—I made some mistakes at first," Elam admits. "I do things differently now than I did when I first started. But I didn't make that many mistakes that I failed," he emphasizes, saying that he learned quickly enough "to stay afloat."

Elam, in his late twenties and running a company for five years, is street-savvy and a quick study. His approach may work, if you are quick enough to pick up what you lack, or get others to show you. It is not for everyone. "I would rather see a person start part-time, and learn not only how to do the work but how to run a business, before they do it full-time," says Isaac Smoker.

Quite a few Amish do just this, continuing to earn steady paychecks while learning and building a customer base.

In Ohio, furniture finisher Harley Stutzman followed this strategy. A bit uncommon for an Amishman, Harley worked on the railroad for a spell and drove a vehicle before being baptized in the Amish church, followed by a stint in a mobile home factory after rejoining the community.

About his chosen trade of furniture finishing: "I had no experience. I just jumped in. It was a little scary, I had two kids at the time, and I had a mortgage payment," Harley explains. "I stayed at the factory when I first started. I didn't leave immediately, and I worked [on the business] in the evenings."

But business grew to the point where "it got to be too much" to hold down both. Today, nearly a decade later, Harley's firm—employing nine members of the community and fulfilling Harley's original vision—could be described as a success in many ways.

Harley's evolution from working full-time to half-and-half to full-time firm owner is a common and sensible example of how many Amish individuals reduce the risk of the start-up while acquiring the know-how and customer base necessary for long-term success.

WHY BUSINESS?

In a nutshell: children, faith, and real estate.

Amish tend to have large families, averaging around seven children per married couple. Significantly, the vast majority of those children tend to remain within the Amish faith.

With an exploding population, land has become scarcer, and—particularly in Eastern seaboard settlements such as those in Pennsylvania or Delaware—pressures created by urbanites fleeing the cities for suburbs and exurbs have caused prices of farm acreage to skyrocket. This has left Amish less able to acquire the 80–100-acre farms they've historically based their lives around.

In order to avoid work in non-Amish environments and to simulate the at-home dynamic of the family farm, small business has become an attractive option. A home business typically requires less start-up capital than a farm, and can be operated part-time while still receiving a steady paycheck.

Additionally, many of the trade skills that the Amish use in their wood-working or homebuilding firms are ones they have long honed on the farm. These labor-intensive, craftsmanship trades are among the most popular for Amish entrepreneurs.

Though both education level and cultural acceptability limit the scope of businesses, one still finds a diversity of firms represented in the Amish business roster. In addition to trades based around the wood and building industries, other Amish enterprises include horseshoeing operations, machine shops, market stands (some operating in urban areas such as Philadelphia or Washington, D.C.), quilt-making businesses, dog breeders, bakeries, dry goods stores, and buggy builders.

Around the edges are a host of less-common pursuits, such as physical therapy, bookkeeping, horse training, herbal medicine, auctioneering, the occasional tourist-oriented businesses providing meals or even stays in Amish homes, guinea pig "farms," and even alternator and engine repair shops, in an example of an unusual meeting of cultural worlds.

PROPER EXPECTATIONS

An important part of the start-up calculus lies in recognizing and evaluating challenges—both physical and mental. Successful business owners are typically paid at an above-average level because of above-average sacrifices of sweat, nerves, or brainpower.

Harley Stutzman explains that "you have to be very determined and focused. If you like a lot of free time, starting your own business is not for you."

His tone attests to the seriousness of his experience. "I didn't see my kids.... I think I did the right thing. I'm glad I did what I did. But I wouldn't want to do it again," Harley admits, citing as especially challenging the times "when you need groceries, and you need supplies for the baby, and the money's not there.

"We never went hungry, but we did with a lot less."

Another of Harley's peers in the trade reflects a sentiment felt by most at some point, when he mentions "A.M." starts—meaning even 2 A.M. in his case. "When I was down there by myself in the morning," he says, "I'd think, '*Why* did I ever do this?' " Short nights and shoestring spending are a common reality. If it ends up not being as big a struggle as expected, call that a bonus.

As we'll examine in the next chapter, mentors and a support structure can be very important during early days. At the same time, entering the business-arena demands independent thinking, which means things can get lonely.

One longtime Amish business owner, no stranger to success, describes the initial reaction of his peers toward his entrepreneurial plans as terrible. "I was the black sheep everywhere," he explains. The way he tells it, he found pessimists around every turn. "People are cruel, baby!" he laughs.

"If you read through the Old Testament, that's the way it's always been," the Amishman continues. "We're prone to destroy other people who are successful. We like to do that.

"We like to see people failing that have been successful, because they're arrogant now.... It just gives us a good feeling!" he remarks, flashing a big ironic grin.

While the direct tone may seem surprising coming from an Amishman, this entrepreneur's words offer an insight on human nature, one which can perhaps explain tax-the-rich cheerleading, corporate scapegoating, and the satisfaction Main Street takes in watching Wall Street titans topple.

Though spoken with tongue at least partially in cheek, the Amishman's take points up a reality: a budding entrepreneur can't always count on emotional support, even from his own community. The people whose opinions you care about most may be the quickest to put you down.

Sometimes the critical eye comes in good faith. You should probably listen to skeptics when it's the trusted and experienced doing the talking. Other times, true motives for raining on your parade may be closer to what this Amishman describes.

Discerning whom to listen to while withstanding naysayers is a common challenge for entrepreneurs and executives. Not everyone will love you or your idea, especially when it's unproven or unusual. Part of running a firm is getting used to kickback and, in some cases, punching ahead regardless.

Sadie Lapp, a pioneer entrepreneur in the Lancaster settlement, describes similar challenges. Though female-owned businesses—often craft- or food-oriented, or smaller-scale cottage industries—are not unheard of today, starting up in the early 1970s Sadie was one of only a few—female or, for that matter, male—Amish operating an enterprise. The Amishwoman admits she encountered "a hard time" from some in her community when starting up her quilting business. Sadie explains that while church leadership was understanding of her desire to open a company, they felt it important that her business be located in the home, reflecting universal concerns over the importance of family.

Today, some Amish females do own prospering companies, though traditional roles persist. Female entrepreneurs are more likely to be single or married and childless, or to have children already grown. Some run full-time operations generating a sizeable income, while others may have sideline affairs. The demands of home and family limit the latitude with which Amish females can operate. Sadie, whose company quickly achieved sales of hundreds of quilts per year, explains that she is happy that she was compelled to operate her business from home, as it allowed her to be around while her children were small.

Gender issues aside, novices sometimes approach first forays into entrepreneurship with a mind-set unanchored in business realities. Some start with the notion that putting up a few ads, picking out a fancy office, and putting on a grand opening will do to get customers rolling in.

The reality is often the opposite. "You gotta go out and look for work instead of waiting for it to come to you," says Ohio Amishman Jon Schrock. This may mean working the phones or flat-out pounding the pavement. It may mean offering initial work or early sales for free or at cut rates.

Considering the typically large investment of toil, trouble, and money, some Amish businesspeople also stress establishing a realistic time horizon and knowing when to cut losses. Having a logical plan removes emotion and minimizes guesswork in decision-making.

Jon finds it useful to set a reasonable time frame. Speaking from experience acquired running successful firms in a pair of industries, he explains that "the first three years in the business is the toughest years" and that "you can't expect to make too much money." If you're still not doing well after a certain allotted time, "then you have to make adjustments."

Those adjustments could be drastic or may even mean calling it a day. Time frames—three years, five years, one—will, of course, vary.

"There's businesses that go in, and the first year they make money, and they keep making money. But that wasn't the case with my business the first two to three years. . . . It's kind of a hump you have to get over."

What will your budget really allow? How will the business affect your lifestyle? What changes will be necessary? And are you being honest with yourself? An accountant's counsel, as well as that of other trusted individuals, can prove useful.

Though support is important, you can't count on universal approval. Negative voices are inevitable. Establish a reasonable time horizon dictated both by financial realities and an assessment of personal commitment. Formulating a vision means taking into account the reality of challenges and kickback as well.

DRIVEN

The underdog, against-all-odds aspect comes pretty much standard to the classic business fable. Early humps and shoestring hijinks make such stories fascinating in the retelling.

The Rubbish Boys, North America's largest mover of unwanted stuff (now under the name 1–800-GOT-JUNK?), was started by a high school dropout in a tight job market with little more than a beat-up, plywood-sided pickup and a tankful of motivation. Hewlett-Packard—and by extension Silicon Valley—famously began in a 12-by-8-foot shed, now a national historic landmark. And the founder of what became Frito-Lay got cooking on a $100 loan from his mother, frying up the first chips in her kitchen and hawking them from his Model T.

Accounts such as these are revisited today with a sense of awe and drama. "The classic business story is much like the classic human story," recounts author Mark Helprin. "There is rise and fall; the overcoming of great odds; the upholding of principles despite the cost; questions of rivalry and succession; and even the possibility of descent into madness."

What intangible qualities does an entrepreneur need to survive? In many cases it's the character and passion of the founder, galvanized by a concrete, all-important vision, that powers the sputtering business through troubled times.

According to some highly successful Amish, sheer inner drive can propel determined entrepreneurs through the early learning phase. And the importance of drive is not to be underestimated. Sadie Lapp had to fight through discouragement that came both from some in her community as well as from a competing quilt seller. Another Amishman admits, "I wanted it so bad, for so many years. . . . To do something like this. I just latched onto it, and it just took off. It's an interesting ride."

When asked about keys to success, veteran Jake Stoltzfus who has nearly four decades in business boils it down to two short words: *"Be hungry."*

Sheer hunger, it seems, can even stand in for other supposedly essential traits. Jake Stoltzfus is a gruff, direct man. Jake is, in a word, intense. He thrives on challenge. He has also become something of a business legend among his people. Early on, Jake did not have to search far for motivation.

"It was easy—pay the bills and feed the family!" Jake explains, reciting a common start-up story. "I had to feed my family; therefore, I had to work, I had to figure it out. There was no other option."

Practically speaking, this meant scrimping on extras—vacations, fancy food, social visits to friends—as well as late nights and near-twenty-hour days. Jake, displaying an inherent penchant for drama, considers the motivation issue simple: "When your back's against the wall, you better come out swinging—or you're gonna starve."

Drama aside, Jake views entrepreneurial hunger—of the type that can't really be learned so much as inspired, absorbed, or self-realized—as the main driver in founding and developing successful firms. He also sees lack of this desire played out in a common generational scenario. In the typical story line, the founder builds the company up from scratch. The second generation lets it stagnate. And in the third, "it goes down the toilet."

Similar tales of entrepreneurial decline play out again and again, even with the benefits, typically enjoyed by inheritors of family firms, of money and a business culture upbringing.

Describing characteristics of a "natural businessman," Jake emphasizes drive above all else. "Most businessmen do not consider themselves successful.... They never reach the goal," he explains, providing a glimpse into the driver mentality. "They don't ever say, 'Ah, I'm successful; now I stop.'"

Amish have differing views on business success. Becoming satisfied with success can be poisonous, according to Jake. Getting fat and happy means "you lost it, it's going downhill," he assures.

Yet, many of Jake's contemporaries, despite working hard for their success, would shy away from his hard-charger approach.

Numerous Amish make a "contentment mentality" an integral part of their visions, essentially self-limiting their firms to fit in with traditional Amish tendencies toward the small-scale and manageable. According to such thinking—and though it may sound heretical to some—learning to be satisfied with a measure of success is actually an integral part of *being* successful.

The money may be great. But in this view, if the push for profit and all it entails causes stress, discontent, and damage to your relationships, then you're missing something. *Success* also means knowing how to handle it, and how to be happy with accomplishments.

This tension between the impulse to expand and the desire to self-limit size in order to better realize a vision is something that many Amish grapple with.

For businesspeople attuned to the "growth is great" paradigm, the idea of limiting size is one that might never enter the picture. But managing growth can be key to modern business success as well. And not just on the level of personal vision. Carefully managed expansion can mean preserving attributes core to the identity of the firm, for example, or could be crucial to maintaining quality.

Growth can also come in ways besides upping production or payroll. Sometimes it simply means getting better at what you do—efficiency enhancements or improved quality, for example.

Modern companies with histories of restricting production in order to preserve brand prestige or in deference to production realities, ranging from motorcycle builder Harley-Davidson to luxury watchmaker Patek Phillipe, testify to the importance of self-limitation. Being mindful about how you grow, and to what degree, can also play into preserving a "family" culture, even in larger corporate settings.

Regardless of the motivation—personal or business-strategic—controlling growth has a real place in the business context. We'll make a further exploration of managing growth, the varying definitions of success, as well as the challenge of fitting a business into a life in Chapter Eight.

Hunger can make up for a lot. Honest self-examination can shine light on your own drive. At the same time, in a consumption-driven world, limitation and contentment are learned traits and not necessarily blasphemous ones in the context of business success.

THE TROUBLE WITH "THE AMISH"

When referring to America's best-known plain community, both scholarly and popular commentators use the term "the Amish" freely, though in fact it falls a bit short.

In truth, the Old Order Amish world is a diverse one. Diversity has emerged for a number of reasons, often having to do with the fact that the Amish are a highly congregational group. This means that there is no "Amish pope" with all-encompassing authority. As a result, groups with differing cultural characteristics have emerged under the Old Order umbrella, one that covers over 1,700 individual congregations across America and Canada.

While all Amish adhere to certain doctrines and beliefs such as nonresistance and adult baptism, peering through the magnifying glass reveals stark differences across the Amish spectrum.

Among other things, Amish vary in degree of conservatism, acceptance of technology, and appearance of clothing, homes, and transportation. Some Amish homes, for example, mimic suburban estates, while others seem closer to ramshackle turn-of-the-century dwellings.

Amish buggies may be black, gray, brown, yellow, or white. In some communities, Amish drive only carriages without a top cover, which can present challenges in inclement weather.

Amish differ in degrees of openness to the world as well. Many are naturally welcoming and interactive with outsiders, and intercultural friendships are common. On the more conservative end, others may be less apt to engage non-Amish neighbors or visitors or to subscribe to the local paper, for example.

In very rare cases, a few allow telephones and even electricity in the home, but the vast majority keep both at arm's length—with phones, for example, safely out in the shop or at the end of the lane in specially constructed shanties. The cell phone, meanwhile, has snuck into a number of communities while remaining mostly absent in others.

Amish businesspeople, typically closer than their farming peers to the non-Amish world, may take a more progressive stance on an issue than their agricultural counterparts would, as may Amish living in larger settlements with more frequent contact with outsiders, versus those in smaller, often more isolated and conservative ones.

Differences are most obvious across *affiliations,* the term for groups of churches that associate closely with one another. The most conservative, for example, differ in notable ways from the more progressive, though groups from opposite ends of the spectrum rub elbows in some areas and may be indistinguishable to the layperson. Most of the Amish who contributed to this book could be classified within the largest affiliation, a "mainstream" subgroup of the larger Old Order Amish family that is, somewhat confusingly, also termed "Old Order" Amish.

Still, for simplicity's sake, serious and casual observers, as well as the Amish themselves, tend to rely on the wide-net term "the Amish."

THE GIFT OF TRYING TIMES

Ivan Miller, a wholesaler operating in a wide-reaching coast-to-coast market, has reached success in the business he founded fifteen years ago on his Ohio farm. Ivan's journey, however, has not been a smooth one. The jovial Amishman hit two stumbling blocks early on: "No experience, and I did not ask for a lot of advice.

"The harder I tried to show people what I was, the more I showed 'em what I wasn't," Ivan admits, humbled at the recollection. Now, he feels, "it's more important to know what you don't know than what you know." On realizing his error, Ivan says, "then I started asking people for advice, that I should've . . . years before," although, he laughs, "I'm still paying for some of my education."

Ivan learned the hard way that with proper planning, study, and consultation beforehand, business start-ups can reduce errors. But inevitably, owners and managers make mistakes. Challenges and obstacles arise, independent of the moves you make or knowledge you possess.

"If you can stay in for the lows, you can do well in the highs" is how Pennsylvania entrepreneur Daniel King sums up his thinking on challenges. "I'm convinced that if we would always have a high, that we wouldn't learn to be efficient," he says.

"But if we have a low," Daniel feels, "it then stimulates—or educates—us to be efficient, when things pick up." Daniel points out the importance of this concept, not just regarding business challenges but in "all kinds of crisis." General-life issues come into play here as well: "You need to have a crisis to . . . be a strong person."

Daniel's words resonate particularly today, in the aftermath of the late 2000s global economic crisis and the governmental and public response to it.

Observers of modern society lament that we have learned to shun pain, struggle, and difficulty as hostile to "the good life." We want ours—and we deserve it, for that matter—and if it entails any extraordinary degree of hardship, we're not interested.

On the contrary, as Daniel explains, a dose of discomfort is often just the "stimulus" needed to grow and to escape stagnant modes of thinking and unproductive behaviors. In lieu of hand-holding and subsidized failure, sometimes a solid kick in the tail is just the tonic an individual or company requires.

"If you get into a low time," Daniel explains, "you can look at this as . . . giving me an opportunity of sharpening my pencil, tightening the belt, and staying competitive, even at low times," he points out. "Instead of saying, 'well, you know these times are just rotten,' and [having] a bad attitude on what's happening."

Daniel recalls an anecdote about a tree, one which ends up putting down roots in response to gusty conditions. "He was a strong tree, *because* of the wind," Daniel explains. If he were protected at all times, "he would not have grown to be as strong," he says. "That's what we need to do in business."

Daniel agrees that this concept can be hard for new entrepreneurs to stomach. Survival in such cases may come down to simple perseverance. "It's not like the minute you're running into the red, that you're going to give up. Because there's numerous others going down the road at the same pace, that are now going to maybe say, 'I'm tired of it. I'm not going to do it.' And eventually that market will pick up again."

The idea that hard times are acceptable, and should even be welcomed, may seem counterintuitive. But the sentiment meets sympathetic ears in Amish society. The capacity to persevere through low periods is rooted in Amish agricultural tradition, with its historical ups and downs and reliance on uncontrollable factors such as weather patterns and milk and crop prices.

Being able to weather hard times results not only in a stronger company and character but in credibility as well. Talking of a once-ruined businessperson who subsequently changed his own fortunes and achieved substantial success, entrepreneur Ezra Miller points out that "he was on the low end, and now he's on the high end. And I can appreciate someone like that.

"He's been on both teams, and that's good," Ezra explains. "The guy that always did well?" Ezra asks. "Not the guy to get your answers [from].

"Because a lot of them are gonna fall sometime," Ezra points out. "And some people when they fall, they think they can't get back up. But you gotta be able to get back up and keep running."

Being able to fall. Just like the rest of America, Amish have had to weather slowdowns in the economy and in some of their key industries.

Along the way, the philosophy of businesspeople such as Ezra and Daniel has no doubt been tested. The blessings of hard times can be tough to appreciate. But sometimes, a gut check comes at just the right moment, and to just the right person. Failure is often just what we need to bring us back down to planet Earth, as Ivan Miller found.

With hindsight, Ivan feels his early struggles have even helped him to empathize and be more of a servant to others. "I feel I can help a lot more people now pull through the tough times, because of mistakes I've made," Ivan explains. "Sometimes when things go tough in the beginning, you have more heart for your people you deal with later on.

"And if my customers have tough times, I can feel for them. I don't just act like they're stupid.

"At the same time," says Ivan, "when something is supposed to be, God can make it happen."

FAITH MATTERS

The famous Amish pragmatism is balanced by spirituality. Ivan's comments reveal an element which features prominently in the visions of many business owners in his community—faith in a higher power.

In Amish America, God is ever present: from morning devotions through bowed heads at lunch to prayers on knees at night, faith manifests itself in concrete ways in the day-to-day.

God's benign hand works in all facets of existence. Amish commonly cite God's providence as essential to their success. In some cases, the language they use even concedes ownership to the Man upstairs. "It's not really my business. I just work here," says entrepreneur Sylvan Miller.

Giving thanks is the default Christian behavior and one that meshes with Amish emphasis on humility. But being human, even Amish struggle with pride at times. Entering the arena of business—where individual decisions are rewarded and personal business acumen esteemed—has sharpened the threat of this deadly sin in a traditionally self-effacing culture.

"Once the human being can do as he pleases, which money often allows you to do, he becomes corrupt," warns another business owner. Aware that some of his peers have at times been distracted by worldly gain, he remarks that "of course, we all wanna go to the same place.

It's the ultimate goal. That is when success becomes a four-letter word, if it might actually get in the way."

Being of strong faith brings many benefits—though business advantage is clearly not the wellspring of Amish piety. Among the tangential benefits of strong faith are a lessening of emotional burdens, a sense of groundedness and security, as well as guiding perspective.

Harley Stutzman, recounting struggling with low sales numbers early on, recalls that "there was times when I'd go home from work, and just think, I don't know if I can do it anymore, and I'd say 'Lord it's all yours, show me the way,' and you'd come in the next morning and here's some products showing up again."

Though falling short of a thinking which presupposes earthly payback for piety, strong faith instills a confidence that efforts will ultimately be rewarded. "I could tell you some stories where things just fell into place. I had no idea where to turn. I just decided I'm going to turn this over to the Lord," suit maker Sylvan Miller explains, describing times when troubles seemed to work themselves out.

In the Amish worldview, faith in God lightens burdens—if not materially, then at least mentally. "There was so many incidents, that I feel without His help I could not have done it," adds Sylvan.

Amish are also aware that though they may act with free will, in the end someone else holds the cards. Among Amish, there's a real sense of submission and of ceding the ultimate picture to a higher power. "We don't know what's gonna happen two years down the road. He might need to teach me a lesson. . . . I don't know," Sylvan concedes.

A Pennsylvania business owner emphasizes that "Whatever he lets happen is probably for the best. Maybe you're looking at a big job, and you don't get it. And that's frustrating," he admits, especially after committing one or two months of work to winning the deal.

But "you need to stop and think, 'maybe I wasn't supposed to have that job.' My prayer is usually for Him to let us have the jobs that He wants us to have."

At the same time, Amish admonish those who kick back and wait for riches to rain down from on high, or those who act irresponsibly and still expect rewards. "So far, if there was a need, it was met," says Sylvan Miller. "But I can't just go spend money; you still have to manage."

Or as one gazebo manufacturer puts it, paraphrasing from Scripture: "We can ask for stuff and pray for stuff, but if we don't take any action, it can't be fulfilled. We're being slothful.

"If we ask for something," he continues, "God expects us to go and do it, make a move on it. If you pray [that] you want to move this hill, you're going to have to make an effort to move it. That's kind of the way we're motivated here."

HAVING VISIONS

The driving desire to start off on one's own frequently springs from dissatisfaction. In such cases, real-life concerns are often the catalyst: higher pay, more free time, more control over one's life. Others gravitate toward business for higher-minded motives, such as solving a persistent consumer problem with a new product or service, creating jobs for fellow community members, or providing a family setting for work.

Well-defined goals and a meaningful, ingrained business vision are an essential part of running a prospering company. Pessimists, setbacks, and subpar early results all serve to discourage beginning businesspeople, and sometimes even prove fatal. A deeply rooted vision assists owners at all stages of their business lives, acting as an engine to power the individual through obstacles and on to achievement.

In many cases, the vision comes before specifics have been hammered out. "I was just about sure somebody could make it work.... How it was all gonna work out, I wasn't sure, all the details," one Amishman explains. But he had a good enough idea of what the final result should look like in terms of his business and the way his and his family's life fit into it.

Today his firm is a success, and you can read the satisfaction on his face; he takes pride in providing a service and employing a healthy handful in his community.

Your vision depends on you and reflects your personal drives, desires, and values. And you don't necessarily need a grandiose world-altering goal or a chorus of angels and trumpets to know a vision has arrived.

Gary Erickson, founder of Clif Bar, envisioned a better-tasting energy food during a 175-mile "Epiphany Ride," and was driven to take his all-natural athletic treat to others who'd also suffered the "unappetizing" and "hard to digest" workout snacks common at the time. Erickson sought to solve a common, nagging problem and in the end created a product that has made life better in a small way for scores of fellow sports enthusiasts.

Some Amish goals reveal a drive rooted in the appeal of challenge. One long-term business vet is selling his original firm and purchasing another, which had declined over a number of years. "It's boring if you have nothing to do. I cannot stand that."

He realizes it will take work to manage the new firm back to profitability. "That's a challenge. I like that. Now I can take something that's been screwed up, and build it up. I have no doubt that it can be done."

Some point to family. Another Amishman, speaking of a large investment in a market-stand business, calls being able to work with family the "number one reason" he became involved. "They were very much enthusiastic about it, and without my wife—without her support—I could never do it."

He also cites the possibility of his sons taking over the business in the future, nodding to the typical Amish desire to create something transferable to future generations. Similarly, a veteran points to a lack of desire on the part of his children to continue as a main reason for shutting his doors. "If you don't have family that wants to keep on going, then there's really no use having it anymore."

Other goals are more down-to-earth, sometimes literally: "I think the biggest thing was to get out of hauling manure," explains Ivan

Miller. "When I was a young man sitting at home plowing, I would sit back down to plow and think, what in the world can I do in life to make a lot of decisions in a short time?"

Whatever it may be, make it your own. As we've seen in these examples, business owners formulate a vision based on diverse motivations. It could be making money and mentoring people. It might be tapping into a new market to provide a product that fulfills a need and improves lives. Or it may simply mean becoming the best in your particular field in the face of challenges and naysayers.

Regardless of what your vision reflects—challenge fulfillment, family focus, a ticket off the manure train—the point is to have one. We'll reexamine vision and the big-picture context in greater detail in Chapter Eight.

So let's assume you have a clear vision in mind.

In the next chapter, we take a look at how Amish, with education ending at eighth grade, equip themselves with the knowledge and skills needed to bring vision to fruition—and at the insights their unorthodox approach to learning can reveal for modern-world managers, experienced executives, and budding entrepreneurs alike.

TEN POINTS ON VISION AND CRISIS

1. A personal business vision can be a powerful driver. Success is possible without one, but when it comes to reaching personal fulfillment and surviving challenges and problems, a deeply held, authentic vision can transform a grind into a vocation.

2. Vision can concern itself with market-oriented goals, but it necessarily includes the personal element—the role you play and the function your business fulfills in your personal and family life, for example.

3. Knowing how to make something or execute a task well doesn't mean you're set to run a business. Technical skill and managerial acumen are two different things. Honest assessment coupled with training and outside advice can help remedy managerial deficiencies.

4. It can be wise to spend time thinking through potential challenges—financial, emotional, or physical—and the real-life impacts they may have.

5. Support from outside is a luxury, not a given.

6. Successful business owners often exhibit one key trait—drive—rooted in a strong desire to accomplish a well-defined goal or vision. Developing and nurturing a powerful vision can help overcome inevitable challenges.

7. Challenges and trials are not necessarily negative. Sometimes we need the hard times to get better at what we do.

8. Amish take strength from their faith. You may, too. If not, what other reserves of strength will you tap?

9. Vision typically begins to germinate well before the ironed-out, tidied-up final plan.

10. Vision is individual and personal. It belongs to you and those you choose to share it with. Whatever it may be, make it your own.

CHAPTER TWO

GETTING SMART

Hands-On Versus the Hallowed Halls

You find these people that will not seek advice.
And they always have to learn the hard way.
—AMISH HARNESS MAKER

I nside the one-room schoolhouse, the young prepare to one day assume the roles of their fathers and mothers—as parents, congregants, and productive members of Amish society.

Other than an Old German alphabet hanging over the board, and a somewhat antiquated appearance, the Amish classroom in many ways resembles its modern counterpart. Hand-scrawled crayon artwork. Multiplication tables. A gallery of presidential heads peering from a sidewall.

All eight classes squeeze into one room, as once was common in rural communities across the nation. The teacher, almost always a young female member of the community, takes on two grades at a time, first reviewing basic numerals and sums then on up to more complex calculations. At math time, "scholars," as Amish call school-age children, approach the front in twos and threes. Others lean over desks, hard at work.

The children toil diligently until the first break at 10 A.M. Then, a welcome respite: softball.

In the room today are future farmers, factory workers, business owners, and housewives. But no doctors or lawyers, no concert

27

pianists-to-be or superstar athletes. At least not if these scholars choose the path of some 80–90 percent of their peers and remain Amish—a choice which, by virtue of cultural norms as much as educational limitations, makes such occupations taboo.

Amish sometimes take heat from the "enlightened" public for their eight-grades-and-out educational program. Such criticism is often flawed. Observers who look down their noses at the Amish approach frequently assign their own values to a culture based around different ones.

Institutional learning has brought vast benefits. Amish, like modern Americans, have been beneficiaries, a fact they typically acknowledge. Yet though Amish appreciate trained professionals such as dentists and doctors, whose services they patronize out of necessity, in the classic Amish worldview, extended formal education is anything *but* a panacea.

"I have nothing against higher education and college," says one long-term Amish entrepreneur. "But I see that as having been detrimental to our country. You lose too many core values. You lose too much common sense," he insists.

Checking himself, he admits his statement may have been a bit too broad, and acknowledges the necessity of formal education in some fields. But at the same time, many Amish sympathize with a common sentiment—that the theorems and case studies of the hallowed halls come up short against hands-on know-how acquired in the real-world arena.

Citing another of his peers, he explains that over those crucial eight years of childhood and early adolescence, "we go to school to learn how to learn."

Skepticism about institutional learning is not unique to the Amish. The founders of modern-day behemoths such as Apple, Facebook, and Virgin lack a college, and in some cases, high school degree. Not to mention the bosses of a host of smaller firms as well. In fact, as Steven D. Strauss, author of *The Small Business Bible*, points out, of the twenty-six million small companies in America, it's more likely than not that the average small-firm owner does not have a college degree either.

Admission to Amish society may be restricted, but there's no magic "business gene" floating around the Old Order genetic pool. The Amish are people of normal intelligence and capability, plugged into a system that consistently produces scores of successful entrepreneurs. Amish simply seek their know-how in places other than Wharton or Harvard.

Ultimately, Amish education is grounded in pragmatism and reflective of shared values. But despite some practical mathematics— checkbook balancing, for instance—the Amish get little formalized business training.

So in the journey from eighth-grade graduates to business success stories, there's a need to plug holes. Amish do this in three highly practical ways: hands-on training; supplemental reading and carefully selected help from business courses and consultants; and by tapping into the wisdom of trusted mentors and peers.

In this chapter, we'll explore how the Amish become successful businesspeople—while bypassing more formalized systems of education some might see as indispensable—and what insights the approach of the Amish holds for the rest of us.

HARD TIMES AT AMISH U

Rather than jet off to B-school, Amish head out back—to the shops and sheds tucked away behind shutterless homes scattered throughout rural America.

And training starts early—as soon as the youngsters are old enough to wander back into the barn, where Dad pounds away on a side project, such as a buggy or a table for Grandma. The youthful trainees, eager to mimic their parents, unwittingly absorb a healthy work ethic just by hanging around *Dat* and *Mam*.

Many Amish learn as adolescents and adults while on first jobs. Amishman Elam Peachey, who spent some years working for a contractor before setting out on his own, epitomizes the always-learning, always-attentive businessperson.

When I sit down with Elam on a sunny February afternoon, he's nearly as eager as I am to talk, with many questions of his own. "I agreed to this interview," Elam explains, "but I also thought that while we're at it, I'm gonna learn some ideas from you—I try to learn from everybody I get in contact with."

Elam has had to apply what he's learned in a changing business landscape. Construction has been a boom industry in Elam's native Lancaster County for much of the past two decades, as a naturally expanding population and a rural locale which pulls in urban exiles has made the area a highly desirable place to live. As a result, some contractors found themselves with more work than they could handle.

"We turned away three-quarters [of business] and did one-quarter," Elam explains, recalling the flush era. But Lancaster has not been immune to the national downturn, which has pinched many local contractors. As a result, Elam has shifted from the new-construction focus into what he sees as a more promising market, the remodel industry.

Like many of his peers, Elam has weathered trying times at the start as well as today. The Amishman gained a lot from the experience of working for another builder and leading a crew.

On the job, knowledge comes from observing others, not just personal experience. "The guy I worked for before, I tell him that I learned an awful lot from him," another Amishman explains. "Some how to do, and some how not to do!"

HANDS-ON

Among Amish, work is perceived as a universal good. Not that you won't hear the occasional job-site grumbles or lack of enthusiasm about getting up early.

It's just that the act of working—with its community aspect and often outdoor setting—can be a rejuvenating, psychologically rewarding pastime, bestowing feelings of productivity and accomplishment.

As many Amish start formal work in some capacity upon finishing school—sometimes at home on the farm, or up the road in an Amish-owned shop—they often enjoy the advantage of ten years of experience or more in a given field before setting out on their own.

This early start gives Amish a leg up on learning the technical side of a trade, and for the motivated and curious, the managerial side as well. Hands-on experiences before going on one's own vary from a single summer spent painting to over a decade crafting chairs by a pair of furniture-making brothers.

One Amishman spent twenty-one years at his previous company, learning the ins and outs and rotating between various positions such as accounting and sales. The skills he learned have helped him run his own profitable firm over the past decade.

"I learned a lot … both ways," he explains. "Things that you should do and things that you shouldn't do. And we try to keep that in mind," he explains, referring to the approach he and his co-owner brother take: "You know, this doesn't work. Or it *didn't* work; there's really no reason that it should work—so don't do it."

"The faster you work, the more you get done, the more money you make. That's common sense," explains furniture maker Ben Miller. "The guy I used to work for before was not like that.

"I loved working for him. But if I was the boss, I would have changed stuff." On opening his own firm, Ben did just that.

A LEARNER'S ATTITUDE

Abe Knepp, the non-Amish owner of K and K Industries, sent his 120 workers home just after getting the initial warnings. Half an hour later, the entire fifteen-building complex was little more than rubble.

The F3 tornado, which hit this Indiana Amish community in mid-November 2005, destroyed over one hundred homes and nearly two dozen businesses. The community response was remarkable. Neighbors rolled up their sleeves and jumped in to rebuild. Men hammered and sawed while women and youth cooked or cleared debris.

Six weeks on, families were preparing to move into nearly finished homes. K and K was back after six months. At an anniversary thanksgiving dinner, Knepp gave gratitude for God's "miracles" and "the many blessings we've received through this."

The tornado strike was not a time to play victim, but an obstacle to overcome. And the response, fairly typical of Amish, bore witness to a few important concepts—thankfulness, positive attitude, and humility. The same spirit is critical for the business owner.

Truth be told, tornadoes, at least in business, are often self-inflicted. Dealing with your own and your employees' errors in an uplifting way—turning pitfalls into blessings and extracting long-term lessons—takes both the proper mind-set and a plan to prevent them in the future.

As one Amish builder put it, "One of the employees ... made a mistake [on the job]. He said, 'I'm still learning.' I said, 'The day you tell me you're not learning anymore, I think we've got a problem.' You're always going to be learning. That's how it is for me."

Elam Peachey emphasizes the active focus required to prevent recurring problems. "Some of your guys will learn from their own mistakes. And some of your guys need help from you to learn from their mistakes. And also you have to learn from your own mistakes, as a leader," he adds.

"You don't ever get your diploma and say, 'I'm finished. I'm done learning.' ... You always learn. You never stop. Until the day you quit, you're gonna be learning new things, hopefully. Or if you believe that you will, you will.

"And if you think you're done," Elam says, "you probably are.

"Even if there's more out there to learn," he elaborates, "you're probably done learning it." The result is that "it might mean you stay at the same income level, and the same place. Which, if that's what you want, that's fine."

And whether that's fine to you or not depends in large part on your personal vision, of course.

Hands-On Learning

Doing can teach in ways that books cannot. Getting practice in a field before starting on your own is wise. And that doesn't have to mean decades: a short, focused spell may be enough to provide insight and plug skills gaps.

Mistakes and challenges become blessings if you choose to see them that way. But the point is to actually *learn* from them. One Amish entrepreneur feels each error should be "unique," and professes "a zero tolerance level for a succession of identical mistakes."

Learning also means leaving your comfort zone. Which usually means seeking the company of people better than you. As we'll examine next, the Amish take advantage of the rich knowledge pool present in their communities.

PRIMITIVE LEARNING?

Why stop at Grade 8? Amish limit schooling for a number of reasons but largely based on grounds of practicality and belief.

While some attend public school, and a few are home-schooled, the one-room schoolhouse is the most frequent venue for educating Amish children.

Amish typically see the knowledge on offer in high schools—often promoting critical thinking and abstraction—as incongruent with everyday Amish life. As they take a literal view of the Bible, secular education can run counter to core beliefs.

Much criticism of the Amish is rooted in the idea that they unfairly restrict their children's future prospects. Old Order education expert Karen Johnson-Weiner responds by saying, "The Amish stifle their children to the same extent we stifle ours with our expectations for their education," while noting that "each culture educates its offspring to perpetuate the culture."

Johnson-Weiner points out that "many Amish might say that we short-change our children by expecting them to learn important lessons from books" instead of "working with their parents and others in the community to contribute in a real way to their families and the church."

Regardless, some Amish hear the call of institutional education from a young age. This can factor into the decision to be baptized into the church, usually made in the late teens or early twenties. Certain individuals raised in the culture have cited hunger for learning as a main motive in leaving their communities behind.

Some businesspeople interviewed for this book admitted that in different circumstances higher education would likely have appealed to them. Active education continues in many venues in Amish society, however, with books and other written resources providing both knowledge and recreation.

TIES THAT BIND

Entering the basement, the only suit and tie in a room of plain coats and frocks, I immediately feel the weight of numerous eyes.

The women and girls, in fresh-pressed head coverings, have been seated for a while. As the men tromp in, a single file of black *mutza* coats and beards, I keep close to my handler, a sixtyish Amishman named Simeon, who walks on just ahead. Simeon leads the way to the hard, backless benches where we'll be spending the next three hours—standard length for an Amish church service.

Simeon isn't really a leash. He's there to guide me through the *Ausbund*—the Amish hymnal—and to translate a bit. Amish church isn't your typical Sunday gathering.

Two tongues prevail this morning: High German, the language of worship, and the English-sprinkled Pennsylvania German, or Pennsylvania "Dutch," which Amish speak as a first language. Amish congregations allow occasional outsiders into their services, but unless they're of similar background, most have a hard time understanding more than the odd word or phrase.

Amish church takes place not in a specially built structure but in and around Amish homes—in basements, barns, and workshops. Economy and a cultural preference for simplicity underpin this practice. Held every other Sunday, service rotates among members' homes. In contrast to other denominations, without a formal building to point to, "church" most obviously means the people present today, gathered to worship God.

Congregants remain largely silent for the duration, except for an unusual drawn-out singing at the beginning and the end. The venerable hymns of the Amish have been passed down for centuries from the time of European forefathers. The opening singing lasts half an hour or longer, after which a solid two hours of preaching, prayer, and Scripture readings will commence. Worship closes with more singing and handling of church matters. It can be long and tiring—dozing off occasionally happens—but it's a definitive piece of Amish life.

Amish society draws strength from the people that comprise it. A church is only as strong as the bonds between its members. Disunity results in disagreement and, in worst cases, church division. Submission and cohesion are prime virtues, and when like-minded members work toward these ideals, the result is a stronger church body.

Similarly, Amish business takes strength from interpersonal ties. The uncles and cousins and grandparents present at church today play a consequential role in the development of budding businesspeople in the community.

They're the ones consulted during the post-worship light lunch or when meeting on country lanes. Adolescents work in their shops, learning how to handle customers and what the numbers are all about. Amish recognize the importance of such entrepreneurial osmosis. "Everybody needs exposure to somebody better than yourself," explains one veteran.

Successful businesspeople must foster and maintain various relationships—with customers, employees, suppliers. One group that's highly important are those that can directly help you learn and grow—mentors, as well as peers in the form of other business owners—both from within your industry and without.

ENTERING A MENTORING RELATIONSHIP

Just how important can those relationships be? Mentors mean "the difference between being successful and failing," according to one Amishman, citing crucial advice garnered from his father-in-law. Though people don't always recognize the help they receive, he contends. "Everybody needs to hear the ringing of the bell."

Mentoring often crosses over from "real life" to the business world. Amish parents model suitable behavior for their children. The lessons last. It's one reason many Amish cite parents as influential mentors. "Everything is so interwoven in business, in life, in church," says another, disparaging the idea of living the Golden Rule on Sundays and "the other six days [being] cutthroat."

An Ohio landscaper credits a more experienced brother for business help. An Amish accountant points to eight years working for a local accounting business, as well as the relationship he's developed with a non-Amish CPA, as crucial sources of insight that he can tap when necessary. A Lancaster variety store owner cites both her parents, who previously owned the business, as well as her own research as crucial sources of knowledge.

Ohio wholesaler Ivan Miller also credits the wisdom he's gained from others over the years. "If you come to a person, and you make them feel that they are way ahead of you in life—that you would really like to glean some of their wisdom—boy, you'll get it."

Ivan offers himself as an example. "Let's say I have an understanding of something, and somebody's really interested in me—I'm happy to share it with them," he declares, proving his point as we sit on the living room couch for yet another talk.

Flattery and appreciation open doors. People tend to share wisdom when it's sought with a genuine heart. Businesspeople are often quite open, perhaps because of the interpersonal nature of business but also because of a natural pride—or rather, sense of achievement—that even the most humble can't help but feel at times.

Seasoned, successful people are all around, if you look. Approaching them with honest interest can open the door to crucial sources of wisdom.

SEARCHING OUT A SOUNDING BOARD

At times, management can be lonely. Decisions are on your shoulders. You're not always sure you're making the right calls.

Elam Peachey points out the valuable capacity of a mentor as a sounding board. Elam feels it's easy to convince yourself of an idea while overlooking flaws and weak points. Outsiders "don't have that prejudice," says Elam. "They're a little more objective."

Elam cites his own informal apprenticeship under his father—a former business owner who ran his first company at age 21—and the insight he's been able to offer. "I didn't always take his advice, but it was still where I went to, to find out."

Still, Elam admits, "it's hard to find a good sounding board."

Besides relatives, acquaintances, friends, and competitors may fill this role. Even a current boss could provide guidance, provided you broach the issue tactfully and with the right person.

Thirty-year business veteran Abram Gingerich has fulfilled the sounding board function for employees considering their own ventures. It can be difficult, especially with top people. "There's only one way to do it—and that is to help them get to where they want to go," while hoping the experience they had on the job "will help them succeed."

Abram tries to be neutral, explaining "the pros and the cons" but maintaining that the decision lies with the individual. He tells counsel-seekers to "get all the facts, talk to some other people, make your decision, and don't look back."

In the search for reliable external ears, Elam Peachey suggests that even employees can be used to sound out ideas, if it's appropriate.

"They're not necessarily included with big decisions," Elam says, but they can be very helpful in improving efficiency and operations on the ground. Employees often have a unique vantage point to assess whether a given change is achieving what it was intended to, and whether other issues have been created as a result.

However, Elam notes one important condition for this to work. "Your employees need to [be] sure that they can tell you something needs to be changed, without thinking that you're going to think badly of them, or retaliate.

"At the same time, it's important to actually ask them, too. Because some guys . . . will know something, and won't tell you, unless you ask them. Just because they don't think you care, or don't have time to listen."

Mentors and sounding boards are important. Sometimes they're one and the same. At other times different people provide these individual functions. They may be found in your family, on your payroll, or even at the business next door. A good manager is open to learning from all sources.

PEER PRESSURE

Many Amish meet peers—in other industries and even direct competitors—on both a formal and informal basis. Business powwows are a chance for camaraderie, accountability, and learning.

For the past five years, Ohio entrepreneur Jon Shrock has met weekly with business-owning brothers and their managers. He says the meetings serve "to keep each other responsible" and "accountable," particularly when they want to improve on specific facets of running their respective companies, including "understanding employees."

Pennsylvania builder Eli King brings a characteristic humility to the learning process. "Once you say you've learned it all is probably about when you're getting started." Eli attends organized business meetings with local entrepreneurs every two months, even after having spent nearly ten years comanaging a company.

"It's always a motivator for me, because most of the members are older than I am," he explains. "They've been in business a lot longer, and I can always learn from them."

Eli cites concrete benefits of the training such as practical com-
munications skills, thanks to public-speaking practice. The skill comes
in handy at the monthly meeting he's recently implemented. Group
speaking is "a lot easier for me now than it used to be."

Lancaster variety store owner Verna Zook maintains contact with
other female business owners at a distance by virtue of an Amish
institution known as the "circle letter." A circle letter is mailed down
a list of recipients, and added to at each stop in its journey before
being sent along to the next. Verna's circle letter group includes
female entrepreneurs in her own state and three others. Circle letters
are a common way to relay information and support in the far-
flung Amish community, and teachers or individuals dealing with
a particular illness, for example, may participate in circle letters as
well.

Ohio native Nelson Mast feels that exposure to others who are
better than you is "the only way you get stretched."

As a young businessperson in the 1970s, Nelson worked as a consultant on an out-of-state business start-up. The experience was crucial
in terms of exposure, as there were few entrepreneurs in his community
at the time. Possibly the greatest impact of this exposure, Nelson feels,
was the effect it had on his confidence.

"I was young, and I was Amish, and being an entrepreneur, I was
intimidated [about] making the right decisions," Nelson admits. "Then
I decided I don't have to be. If they could make decisions that are worth
following, I can too."

Nelson relates the experience to ping-pong. "The only way to get
better is [to] play with somebody better than yourself," he reasons.
"And I played with players a lot better than me."

Mentors and Peer Support

Mentors and peers can be rich sources of knowledge and support.
Getting real benefit requires the humility to acknowledge you don't
have all the answers. Developing mentor or business-peer relationships

takes effort. But sometimes learning real lessons takes stepping outside of what's comfortable and known.

The experienced are often happy to share their insights with motivated seekers. A sounding board fulfills a valuable role and, depending on the issues involved, can be found in many places, not just among the more experienced.

JOINING

For Amish, baptism is a conscious choice.

Becoming a church member—a life commitment—is a momentous step. Amish typically join between the ages of eighteen and twenty-two, though there is no official "cutoff"; occasionally, some commit much later, even approaching age 30.

The youth period *Rumspringa,* translated as "running around," has been a recent surprise entry into American pop culture, thanks to a number of media pieces exploring this formative time. Starting around age 16, the period is marked by an increase in social activity. But the hard-partying Amish teens of some depictions are not the rule.

In fact, "running around" for many Amish is much tamer. Group singings, volleyball matches, and other formal events, often adult-supervised, are the arenas where Amish youth socialize and where matches are made. Like their modern counterparts, Amish youth go steady and may date several people before finding that special someone. Finding a mate, one Amishman explains, is a primary purpose of *Rumspringa.*

Some will push boundaries during this time, often in relatively benign ways, such as by dressing "English," acquiring a driver's license, or even installing an on-buggy stereo, bass thumping over the clatter of hooves. Though wild partying has been a real issue in some communities, it tends to be localized and less common in smaller settlements.

The Amish occasionally attract seekers who eventually become converts. To be married in the Amish church, one must be a baptized member. The rare non-Amish bachelor, smitten with a baptism-bound Amish lass, must think long and hard about taking the plunge, meaning not just a marital commitment but a jump out of modernity into a more demanding existence. Despite the challenges of plain living, a small number of outsiders have become Amish, often for reasons of love, conscience, or both.

Self-motivated seekers make up the bulk of Amish converts. Amish do not evangelize, choosing to focus spiritual efforts on guiding their youth. Though the choice is outwardly free, hopes, expectations, and not-so-subtle pressure can influence the decision—not unlike modern parents harboring spiritual or career ambitions for their own children.

FORBIDDEN KNOWLEDGE?

The meetings were meant to be about business. How to be better.

Some say there were other motives.

By late 2005, when his courses were banned by Lancaster County bishops, Bill McGrane had churned the pot enough to cause some Amish to rethink their religious paths. Some claim that dozens of families left area congregations because of the Kentucky-based business guru's seminars.

Once Amish began exiting the church after attending local McGrane Institute lectures, community leaders became alarmed. "Some people almost considered him the Messiah," points out one Amish attendee of the courses who stayed with the faith. "And then the next people considered him the son of the devil," he chuckles.

The seminars became problematic, wrote Daniel Burke in the Lancaster *New Era*, when focus supposedly shifted from business and finance to topics such as spirituality and sexuality, areas which brought the courses' propagators under suspicion. "It was not about self-help," maintains the Amish lecture-goer. "It was about creating a following." After churches asked their congregants to restrict attendance voluntarily—and were unsatisfied by the response—they banned McGrane's seminars.

Even with attendance by Amish prohibited, the consultant continued to operate. Ultimately, says this attendee, the seminars were a "money racket." "The joke goes that he was better than the salesman who sells ice cubes to Eskimos," he explains, smiling. "He sold horse manure to Amishmen."

Whether McGrane's seminars were useful in a business context or not, suspicion remains when it comes to personal-enhancement training. Some feel the content can run counter to Amish emphasis on harmony and collective good over self-promotion.

Though formal courses may now be all but horse manure to certain Amish, others continue to take advantage of outside means of assistance, at times even provided by members of their own communities.

Despite their caution, Amish recognize that knowledge and skills gaps exist. Many feel that reasonably priced (McGrane's allegedly hit the $5,000-a-week range), ethically sound seminars and courses probably can't hurt—and in best cases can truly help, especially when pinpointed to a specific area of improvement.

Amish entrepreneurs take spirituality into account. It matters that teachings and methods align with Christian values. Religious or not, it's worth considering the ideals propagated by a given course, program, or consultant, and whether they mesh with your own.

In the next section, we'll take a look at external sources of business wisdom, and what Amish seek to gain when taking advantage of consulting services or picking up a business tome.

The importance of outside sources to Amish businesses can be considerable. "Basically, that's the means of education beyond eighth grade," says one Amishman. There can be value for non-Amish as well, of course. Practically speaking, in a changing world, businesspeople who wish to thrive must continually educate themselves, regardless of how much they may already know.

OUTSIDE SOURCES

Twenty-year construction veteran Dennis Miller, born, raised, and baptized Amish, missed his shot at Harvard. "I got out of grade school when I was thirteen . . . and was twenty-eight when I went into business for myself," he explains. "There's a fifteen-year span in between there—you forget a lot of what you learned—plus what did you learn about business in grade school?"

Despite his strong love of the trade, "To make that transition from being a great framing carpenter to being a businessman, with an eighth-grade education, can be kind of difficult."

As a result, Dennis has taken an active approach to his business education: in addition to gaining hands-on experience, he's spent time with books and business seminars. Certain points have stuck.

"If you're in business, the three people you need to be able to be on a sit-down basis with ... are your accountant, your banker, your attorney," says Dennis, citing knowledge gleaned from a book read years ago. "I ask a lot of advice from those people ... especially my accountant." Though "you might not always do what they say," Dennis still values the input.

Dennis claims that many peers are not always so careful to seek advice—including himself, at least at the start—resulting in hardship that could be avoided.

An Amish bookkeeper who advises contemporaries on profitability and business purchase issues says that "a lot of these people had no idea" how much paperwork can be involved in running a company.

He calls himself "a dark cloud" for some enthusiastic business-people who walk into his office. "They might not be as happy when they walk out the door," he explains with a chuckle, though acknowledging that "they need to know that stuff."

Some experienced Amish have begun offering formal and informal consulting for businesspeople within the community. Amishmen contribute to business seminars in both Holmes and Lancaster Counties, offering guidance both practically useful and culturally acceptable.

One talk, entitled "From Farm Boy to Entrepreneur," delivered by a thirty-year business veteran, covers topics with titles such as "Everything I ever needed to know I learned on the farm," "Success can be the biggest detriment," and "Being a team player in your industry."

Others seek help from outside the circle in order to plug cultural gaps. Nelson Mast, the "Farm Boy" of the seminar talk above, relates his experience with marketing to his community's approach to transportation.

"If we're gonna do it right, we have to do [it the] same as we do when we travel. We hire a taxi," he explains. "We use public transportation. We have to sub [contract] it out." Likewise, Nelson feels "that's where the marketing belongs."

Marketing "is a little tough for us Amish," he points out, "because we intentionally refrain from all the styles and fashions. And our mind is set that way."

When first learning marketing, "I was constantly connected with somebody outside our circle." In his case, this meant paying a consultant. "We don't watch TV, we don't know these names, we don't know these fads."

The expense was worth it. "He gave me pointers that lasted for years," says the Amishman. The point may seem specific to the Amish. But being "modern" doesn't mean automatically understanding market segmentation or even how to select an appealing name for a product.

The wisdom here is in recognizing weak points and—if getting personally better at them is unfeasible, unlikely, or too costly—outsourcing them to specialists and experts.

HEALTHY SKEPTICISM

Still, many approach outside help with a skeptical eye. "Books and business seminars are a good approach," reasons Elam Peachey, while cautioning against "paying thousands of dollars a month."

Elam patronized consultants for a time, resigning when he came to feel he was "grossly overpaying." "They make promises . . . they say if your business didn't meet the goals they said it would, it was your fault, and not theirs," a disclaimer he considers "a little shaky."

Another challenge for Amish are the values promoted.

"I started to realize that a lot of the stuff they teach is kind of counterproductive to our Amish culture anyway," he points out. "They want you to act like a bigwig so people think you're a bigwig, where the Amish lessons are humility and just 'stay in your place, you know, don't be a big shot.' "

Another businessperson likens motivational speakers to "caffeine ... once it's wore off, it's wore off," preferring professionals "that speak out of experience." At the same time, others see value. A business owner with an atypical background in network marketing confesses, "I *love* motivational seminars," and says that they "helped me a lot." The benefit, according to him, is in how they help shape productive thinking.

Often, however, the same wisdom may be found elsewhere. "You can read 'love your neighbor' in your Bible," says Elam, "and just go by that.

"The older I get," he muses, "the more I realize that there is an answer in the Bible for just about every problem you're going to have."

Elam claims the key is being "willing to commit yourself to it, and look for it." But "if you'd rather just pay somebody," he adds, "to ... you know, tell you—hey, it's that easy."

THE BIG ONE

In Amish society, one book stands above all. "There's so much wisdom in the Bible about how to run your business. And you can go by that and sleep at night," says one Amish contractor.

Others enthusiastically plug the entrepreneurial and managerial wisdom in Scripture, or at least that pulled from somewhere between the lines.

Amish furniture builder Alan Troyer, describing the Bible as "the number one book that was ever written," retrieves his business card, which features a pair of scriptural quotes. "Those two have helped me quite a bit, to stay focused."

Ohio Amishman Alvin Hershberger also mines the Holy Book for practical knowledge. When it comes to business wisdom, he has a clear favorite. In fact, numerous Amish businesspeople mention one biblical book in particular as especially relevant.

"I wish I could memorize the whole book of Proverbs," he says. "Because there's a lot of truth in there, about business, and about making money, and using money, and handling people," explains Alvin, who also does duty as a minister in his congregation.

By way of example, he points out, paraphrasing a section of Proverbs, that "the 'quick rich' never lasts long. But slowly over time is the best way." Alvin offers a cautionary example "about the person who trusts in a fool," compared in the book to tying a stone to a slingshot.

"Can you imagine [when] you tie a stone to a slingshot, what happens?" he asks. "It comes back and hits you in the face." Whole disciplines can be found within the book, according to Alvin: "Marketing is actually the book of Proverbs."

The Bible is a rich source of wisdom for life and, by extension, business. Its wisdom is often profound in its simplicity. Though simple does not always mean easy.

"My number one thing is the Bible, and the Bible has extremely easy-to-understand Scriptures," says another business owner. "A lot of people try to figure out the hard-to-figure out ones," he acknowledges. "Part of that problem is the easier ones to understand are the toughest to live."

REST OF THE SHELF

Besides the Bible, what else is on the Amish bookshelf?

A variety of reading material is on hand in the typical Amish home, including Amish-produced newspapers, Christian magazines, books on nature and history, as well as religious-themed works. Amish business owners benefit from business-related titles ranging from Zig Ziglar to Peter Drucker, for the more cerebral.

Alan Troyer details a pair of favorites. "One of them is Max Lucado—*It's Not About Me*," says Alan, "and the title pretty well explains what we're here for . . . to bring glory and honor to God."

The second? K. P. Yohannan's *Living in the Light of Eternity*. The Indian-born missionary leader's work challenges readers to reevaluate everyday concerns in the context of "what will last forever." For

Alan, these two works have "really made a difference in the way you think," as well as making you realize that sometimes "you take yourself too seriously."

Manufacturing veteran Abram Gingerich recommends regular exposure to good books. John Maxwell, Stephen Covey, *The Purpose-Driven Life,* and *The Little Red Book of Sales Answers* are favorites, though he remains selective. "There are some that we use, some that [are a] 'I'm-not-sure-that-I-would-go-there' type of thing," Abram cautions.

"It gives you some sense of what works, and what doesn't," he explains. "And I think just reading, even other material . . . gives you a broader perspective on a lot of issues that help build relationships, that help you see the big picture."

At the same time, Abram realizes that books are not the be-all and end-all of a prosperous company. "I know some people that don't read much, and they're still successful. So that's not the only thing it takes."

Another business owner emphasizes that it's important not only what you read but how often. Like many, he uses mornings as a daily scheduled reading time.

The biggest benefit of regular reading of positive materials, Alan Troyer feels, is that "if you keep reading . . . some things will pop up.

"And sometimes . . . it's not a paragraph you read that you can even remember . . . it'll change you, although you don't remember what it was," Alan explains. "So you do live a better life, and you don't know why, but it's because of all the good books you read."

GETTING SMART

The knowledge and skills it takes to run a firm successfully can be acquired in many areas. Institutional learning can have definite value but is only one of many means of preparation. Amish entrepreneurs and managers show that rolling up sleeves, tapping into available human capital, and filling in gaps with books, seminars, and consultants—offering practical lessons and concrete information—are effective ways to supplement skills and knowledge lacking due to experience level or upbringing.

In the next chapter, we'll take a look at how Amish entrepreneurs apply acquired knowledge and skills in bringing their goods to consumers. We'll examine the methods they use to market their products—and themselves—as well as explore insights on selling effectively while respecting the customer.

TEN POINTS ON GETTING SMART

1. A business education can be had in numerous places and be based in numerous resources.

2. Firsthand, hands-on learning can be hard to replicate in the classroom. Real-life participation allows learning by doing and observing.

3. Mistakes—both your own and those of others—are opportunities to learn.

4. Benefiting from mistakes takes analysis and action. Take proactive steps to prevent recurring issues.

5. Outside sources, such as mentors, can be crucial to development. Mentors can impart knowledge and also serve as sounding boards.

6. Peers and even competitors can be crucial to learning, among other ways, by fostering improvement through accountability.

7. Employees can be rich sources of useful ideas. Managers must create an environment where employees feel comfortable contributing without fear of retribution.

8. Outside consultants and professionals can be of benefit, especially when pinpointed to a specific issue. Be sure you are paying within reason and not violating your values.

9. Seminars and books can help as well. Choose material that is useful and applicable to your own situation. Repetition and regularity can be as vital to learning as the material itself.

10. Go for outside help if there is a real and present need and if there is tangible value in filling the need. Plugging gaps in knowledge and ability must be done either by learning it yourself or hiring someone else to handle it.

CHAPTER THREE

MARKET-BOUND

Excelling at Sales and Marketing

If you make something the customer don't want . . . he'll let you know.
—OHIO AMISH FURNITURE MAKER

Alvin Hershberger is spilling the company beans as we sit—cups of homemade grape juice in hand—under the shade tree on the Amishman's farm. Current case: bend over backwards to solve a problem, and customers tend to stick.

"Statistics tell you that . . . if you go above and beyond [to fix something], that customer will be more of a customer than if nothing happens," he explains. Alvin, it seems, has come up with a top-secret strategy to squeeze maximum benefit from the concept.

"So we break stuff on purpose," the Amishman reveals, a cheeky grin spreading across his face.

The jokes come easy for Alvin, a fortyish furniture manufacturer and native of the largest Amish settlement in the world, located two hours south of Cleveland in hilly Holmes County. Alvin is the type who works his tail off, but doesn't take himself too seriously.

Alvin's business is bursting at the seams. The manufacturing facility is due for another expansion. A dozen workers brush elbows moving raw materials in and finished product out to the companion retail shop located on one corner of the farm.

Alvin speaks of an upcoming marketing blitz, a "shock and awe" campaign, as he calls it, backed by a premium catalog, with a price tag well into five figures. Alvin, perhaps showing a bit of a contrarian streak, is confident it will pay off, sensing the time is right, in spite of—or perhaps *because* of—the cramped market and sluggish economy.

The more savvy businesspeople in Alvin's community realize that effective marketing directly results in increased sales. As one of his peers puts it, "People don't realize that if they would market right, sales is easy. There's a huge, huge difference in marketing and sales. You market something right, the people are ready to buy."

Marketing pros divulge wisdom on click-through rates, brand equity, permission techniques, and so on. Marketing departments at some companies employ teams of specialists with multimillion dollar budgets. But what is marketing, exactly? The concept often gets conflated with advertising or selling. Actually, it's neither—though effective marketing works in tandem with both.

The American Marketing Association describes it as "the activity, set of institutions, and processes for creating, communicating, delivering, and exchanging offerings that have value for customers, clients, partners, and society at large."

A veteran Amish entrepreneur defines marketing more simply as "identifying who your buyer is gonna be . . . and making a connection."

It's also "all the service to get [your product] there," he explains, pointing out that "advertising is only one segment of that." To another, it's "connecting to people without talking to them." Modern notions of marketing are often rooted in the idea of relationship-building, in contrast to the single-shot ad campaign.

The successful Amish business owner is acutely aware that he lives and dies by the strength of the relationships formed with employees, suppliers, distributors, and particularly customers. In this chapter, we'll look at the approach of some Amish to marketing—one that prioritizes the interpersonal experience.

The "story" of the typical Amish business holds special attraction for a certain clientele. In the following sections, we'll scrutinize the inherent appeal of Amish businesses and their goods, while examining how any company can discover, create, and emphasize the special elements of its own story in order to maximize appeal.

Following our look at marketing, we'll shift to a crucial stop in the journey from concept to consumer with a look at how Amish do sales—based foremost on an overriding respect for clients.

IN DEMAND

Four hundred miles west of Alvin's homestead lies the midsized Amish settlement at Arthur, Illinois, a welcoming one-stoplight village whose main drag doubles as the county line.

At Arthur, Amish-run shops pop with activity. Marc Olshan reports in *The Amish Struggle with Modernity* that even thirty years ago Arthur had been named "the emerging shop culture" among the Amish. Agriculture remains vital, but the shift off the farm continues. Today, it's safe to say the shop culture here has, in fact, emerged.

For Alvin Hershberger and his counterparts in Arthur and else-where, wood is big business. Building enterprises have sprung up every-where around the heartland town, home to over fifty wood-related firms.

Hundreds of Amish chug away six days a week, many in bustling furniture and cabinet businesses. Arthur wood companies run the gamut of sophistication—from sawmills and pallet makers to custom-design cabinet builders and specialty craftsmen.

Driving around Arthur, you may spot the occasional luxury vehicle planted in front of a Spartan workshop. No, that's not an Amishman gone wild—most likely it's just a big-city buyer.

Customers from Chicago, St. Louis, or Indianapolis make the three-hour trek to this off-the-beaten-path community. Buyers typically wait three to four months for a piece of furniture. For top producers, the backlog of orders can stretch a year or more.

People are willing to spend serious money on Amish goods. An Allen County, Indiana, cabinetmaker describes a single installation costing in the six figures. Handmade hickory rocking chairs might sell for $120 straight from the shop in Holmes County, Ohio, but are priced two or three times higher by catalog and online dealers. Luxury bed frames can exceed $10,000. Other, non-wood goods—foods, home furnishings, or metal crafts—also come at premium prices.

Three-hour drives, premium prices, extended waits. Something special is bringing the outside in to "buy Amish."

THE AMISH STORY

Just what makes an Amish-made coatrack more attractive than a non-Amish one? Seth Godin, author of best sellers such as *Purple Cow* and *All Marketers Are Liars,* extracts marketing lessons from exceptional businesses. Godin asserts that with the purchasing power and vast range of choice available today, consumption is often less about necessity and more about pleasure, novelty, and entertainment.

The challenge of fulfilling humdrum needs has been subsumed by the pursuit of a sophisticated set of *wants,* according to Godin. And crucially, these wants are often satisfied by the stories that we attach to products. "What people want is the extra, the emotional bonus they get when they buy something they love," says Godin.

We "love" products that prove themselves more than just a commonplace commodity. As Godin explains, a product's or business's "story" can be thought of as the associations surrounding it that affirm a pre-existing set of desires, beliefs, and perceptions—or "worldview," as Godin terms it—of the consumer.

Shoppers in Amish Country hunt tokens of rural simplicity to cart home to a hurried urban existence. The quilts and curios they purchase embody values and concepts they may yearn for but find lacking in their everyday lives—serenity, simplicity, a sense of tradition.

Many Amish, few of whom have heard of Godin, are nonetheless quite conscious of the indigenous appeal. A progressively minded furniture maker comments on the promotional potential of his culture: the Amish name is "definitely a plus. People are intrigued with our lifestyle. And that sells."

To a particular breed of buyer, "Amishness" is the whole point. An Amish produce seller near Shipshewana, Indiana, remarked that she needed to be sure that her vegetables come from the Amish, because that's what her clientele expects. At one online outlet (amishcraft.com), visitors learn that

> every item featured on this web site is made by Amish people in Lancaster County, Pennsylvania. The wagon wheels are made by a company that makes wheels for real wagons, and the straw hats are also authentic. The candles are hand-dipped by Amish. Many of the rest of the products are made in converted portions of barns on Amish farms.

A casual scan of related ads and sites reveals that pedigree is the point. Retailers fall over themselves to make it known their wares arrive all but deep-fried in "Amishness."

But for the Amish, promoting core elements like identity and story is not as simple as it may be for modern-world businesses. The progressive furniture dealer reflects on a point of contention in his community. "A lot of people say you shouldn't use the Amish name to sell."

"Well, Amish is not our religion; Amish is our culture," he contends. "Amish people have to realize that. We're Christians," he asserts, etching a firm line between spirituality and society.

More than a few Amish would object to this businessperson's perception of, and willingness to promote, his background. Amish businesspeople large and small grapple with the issue, which has important implications when it comes to marketing their businesses.

LEARNING AS WE GO

Back on his Ohio homestead, Alvin is describing the evolution of marketing in his community.

"Years ago, because of who we were . . . and [knowing there was] furniture in the area, people came here. All you had to do was put a sign out at the end of your driveway that you made furniture, and you were busy."

Some Amish admit that early on, often the "Amish mystique," as it's been termed, used to be enough to bring buyers flocking to the doors. Or as one longtime veteran jokes, "Everybody could make furniture—even if he couldn't!" This was in the so-called golden period of the 1990s, when Amish enterprise boomed.

Now that the economy is down, says this old-timer, "it's separating the men from the boys." In recent years, there has been a small-scale shakeout among Amish furniture makers, whereby some of the less well-positioned operations have closed their doors.

Various other factors helped bring the flush times to an end, including outside competition. "That was before China made furniture, and imports," Alvin explains, citing improvements in quality that he feels have Chinese products approaching the level of Amish-made ones.

Alvin contends that though foreign quality may be improving, "They don't have the service, they don't have the culture, they don't have the connection that we can have."

The many Amish businesses that remain still possess characteristics that attract buyers, including a reputation for quality and the persistent Amish mystique. But as Alvin points out, it's not enough to just sit back and watch business roll in anymore.

Above all, Alvin maintains, "we have to have a connection." Gregarious by nature, Alvin relishes fostering personal bonds with his clientele. Well aware of the rustic appeal of his establishment, nestled in the Buckeye-Appalachia foothills, Alvin pulls out all the stops to make driving down his lane pleasant for all.

Alvin's approach was born largely of necessity. "I knew that if I'm way back in here, I need to have something above and beyond . . . the stores on the main highway. So I felt that if I made the furniture and they could buy directly from the manufacturer, that would help me . . . and that has really been successful," he admits.

Among other efforts, Alvin hosts a yearly anniversary event. His brochures feature a photo of the long picket-fenced lane leading into his picturesque rural sanctuary. Alvin's wife, typical of Amish homemakers, is a master cook, a touch that can't hurt when clients and guests drop by.

"Even though a lot of my furniture gets sold out of state," Alvin explains, "people really love coming in here. People like the idea of . . . seeing the farm, seeing the shop, knowing that [the furniture is] finished here." He speaks of many return visitors, including the company's first-ever customer from nearly a decade earlier.

Alvin realizes that the appeal lies not just in the quality of his products or in the Amish 'mystique' alone, but in the underlying story of his business. The idea of buying directly from an off-the-beaten-path venue can attract furniture shoppers not averse to a bit of adventure. Not every buyer will take this route, but for the ones to whom that story appeals, Alvin provides handmade furniture and an uncommon buying experience.

What makes your business remarkable? Is it the way you sell? A value-add you offer that others don't? The way your products or services get delivered? It's worth thinking through your organization's defining characteristics, even if your market is not as crowded as the one for Amish furniture.

SPREADING THE STORY

Marketers and salespeople underscore the value of their wares when they emphasize ideas and selling points that cater to the consumer's particular set of desires. They accentuate elements of their products, services, and business that connect with concepts, feelings, and ideas which customers hold dear.

Most directly, this is a accomplished through the language surrounding the product—the sales copy, slogans, mottoes, descriptions, and imagery. In the case of Amish marketing, examples abound. Here, a few snippets illustrate how Internet retailers propagate the Amish story:

> Please remember that these pieces of Amish furniture are *treasured heirlooms*. Our skilled Amish craftsmen don't just make furniture. . . . They *build memories*. [Amish Alley]

Rekindle the exuberance of *carefree* childhood with these *old-fashioned* games and toys that will make the kids squeal with delight again. [Amish Acres]

Passed down from generation to generation, folk remedies and *traditions* are not only often effective but inexpensive ways to save a trip to the family doctor. From tea to shining tea, discover the simple wonders of our *heritage*. [Amish Acres]

What does all the drippy wording convey? Buying Amish means an instant piece of "old-fashionedness," a spot of unrestrained rural bliss. Avoid the trouble of creating your own "tradition" or "heritage"—just grab the MasterCard and have some of ours.

Adept marketers can even weave seeming drawbacks into the fabric of the story, reinforcing it. The Branch Hill Joinery, selling furniture made by Michigan Amish, explains on its site that

quality custom craftsmanship does not mean perfection, especially when many hand tools are being used. . . . These minor imperfections do not detract from the functionality of the piece. Many of our customers have remarked that *these small imperfections are exactly what gives our furniture character,* and are also what makes our Amish furniture *more similar to real antiques*.

In one deft sentence the Joinery has transformed production flaws into "character." Not only that, they've lifted Amish furniture beyond mere functionality—suddenly it's just around the corner to antique status.

Some merchants take the concept even further. An Ohio finishing-shop owner points out that flaws now even come built in, noting the increased popularity of "distressed" furniture, nicked and scuffed to appear worn and antique-like. One northern Indiana dealer, in a seeming contradiction of terms, even advertises its goods as "instant heirlooms."

Is there something deceptive or unethical about this approach? Not at all, if the product stands up to what the marketing claims. Character flaws fit with the customer's perception of handcrafted furniture in this case. It's just another thread in the story.

The lesson is that the language in your advertising and marketing copy can be used to evoke qualitative and experiential elements that appeal directly to a certain segment of potential buyers. The crucial bit is identifying those concepts within your business and relaying them to that potential market.

When it comes to Amish furniture, the contrast with the mass-market alternative is striking. The questionable materials and do-it-yourself assembly of big-box furniture retailers tell a different story entirely. In the end, one simple phrase—"Amish-made"—tells a certain group of buyers all they need to hear.

Ultimately, the language you use to evoke your product's selling points—so long as it stands up under scrutiny—often turns out to be just as important, or even *more* so, than the inherent qualities of the product itself.

STORYTELLING

When it comes to making the most of your story, the fundamental task is identifying and spotlighting the remarkable and noteworthy in your product or business. Lack a compelling narrative? Discover or create one.

This may mean altering the way you do business, the way you interact with customers, or even the products or services you provide. Or it may simply mean digging deeper within your existing business to unearth your own unique story.

Your narrative doesn't have to be unique on God's Good Earth. It may just be a simple something that differentiates you in a notable way from your immediate competition.

Selling books to the Amish, I differentiated myself through my relaxed, zero-pressure sales approach. And as one of my wittier Amish friends puts it, there are three main means of communication: telephone, television, and "tell-a-Amish." All are fast as lightning.

Word spread around my market and laid a path in front of me as I approached new Amish prospects. As I met more and more families in these communities, I found that they saw me as the laid-back sales guy who "hardly took up any of your milking time." Sitting down with me meant a fun experience that might even leave you in a better mood than you were in before.

My story was convincing and believable, as I proved it—and promoted it explicitly—at each sales call. Amish themselves, both buyers and non-buyers, commented favorably on the approach. Without doubt it got me in doors that would not have opened otherwise, meaning, of course, more sales.

After you've identified your story, use all your available outlets to make your potential market aware of it. Craft your promotional materials in suitable language. If exceptional customer service is part of your story, make sure the people who answer your phones understand that and know how to convey it from the very first word.

But your story itself is just one element. Needless to say, if no one knows about it, it does you little good. Different businesses rely on different means of making themselves known. Some means—such as the sales copy examined earlier—directly convey elements of your story. Others are designed simply to get a prospect to give you the chance to do so.

In this, some get best results from advertising. Others—many—lean on word-of-mouth promotion, which we'll explore in greater depth in Chapter Four. In the next section, we'll examine two top Amish marketers' success, and the strategies they use to disseminate their messages.

STEALING THE STORY

"Amish" bedsheets. "Amish" turkeys. Even "Amish" software. So just what makes one product "Amish" and another not?

If an item is produced and sold by an Amish person, it would by most lay definitions count as "Amish." But there's a simpler way to reach Plain Nirvana: just stick the Amish label on it, regardless of where it originated. In fact, many operations "steal" the story in this way.

"Amish" sells. Others realize this and jump on board. It's like going to buy the three-stripe sneakers and ending up with the four-stripe knockoffs. Only in this case there is no "copyright" protection to prevent these businesses from calling their products "Amish" outright.

Nowhere is this more evident than in the heavily touristed larger communities. Lancaster County sees over a billion dollars in annual consumer spending, much of it tourist money—ample incentive for outsiders to dip into the cash kettle.

In most cases, those that shout "Amish" loudest usually have little basis doing so. Slap the words "Amish Country" on the package, and run-of-the-mill mixed nuts gain a sparkle—and a chunky markup as well. Restaurants proclaim "Amish-style Cooking" while dishing out cafeteria-style grub. There may be Amish roots in the ownership or Amish waitresses on the payroll, but these are usually not bona fide Amish-owned-and-run operations.

Amish themselves typically do not feature the name, but distributors or retailers often do. Though they recognize the power of the association, Amish are usually not too thrilled when outsiders lean too heavily on the A-word to promote a product. "We feel the Amish life isn't just about how we make things," explains Ohio apple butter producer Naomi Miller. "It's about the faith that we have. . . . And we feel it's not right to use Amish just so we can sell something. Not everybody feels that way."

In practice the strength of the Amish label also threatens to be a weakness. A portion of the buying public perceive Amish companies as part of a single, all-encompassing body, which some Amish business leaders recognize could prove a pitfall should individual Amish neglect quality. Likewise, there is concern about potential dilution of the "Amish" association over outsiders selling shoddy, Amish-tagged goods.

But with no official trademark, and preferring to avoid court, Amish probably won't be rising up against brand hijackers anytime soon.

At the same time, this imitation, borrowing, or thievery, depending on your viewpoint, is also a tribute to the Amish "brand." The Amish story offers undisputable appeal. Free riders recognize this and provide less-discerning buyers with what they see as the real thing.

GETTING THE STORY OUT

Does advertising work?

Ad legend John Wanamaker offered a bit of wisdom in a classic quip. While acknowledging that half his ad money was wasted,

Wanamaker complained that the problem was he didn't know which half.

The answer to the age-old question of whether advertising works is that it depends on what you do, and how intelligently you do it. Forethought and analysis can cut down on the elusive ad waste that plagued Wanamaker and countless others.

Advertising is not a magic bullet. If your product is flawed, throwing money into advertising is not a solution. But as part of a carefully crafted marketing strategy, ads can play an important role in introducing and furthering elements of a company's story.

Abram Gingerich has been honing his marketing for three decades. And like most savvier Amish businesspeople, Abram realizes that advertising alone is just one element of an effective strategy. "We advertise mostly to keep people aware of who we are, where we are," Abram explains.

Abram credits the usefulness of well-crafted company literature to an effective marketing plan. His stated goal when advertising is to get people to order his catalog. Catalog in hand, customers either call in to the company or Abram or his employees follow up by making contact themselves.

Abram acts with an eye to developing relationships for the long term, emphasizing that he searches out "good quality people." "The big part of our business goes out wholesale—we have a dealer network," he explains. "And we really try to take care of them, support them, and help them sell product."

Ads help Abram initiate the relationship. Follow-up in the form of a call or some other personal contact takes it a step further. Without a plan for how to convert an encounter with an ad into a relationship, the impact of advertising is blunted.

With Abram selling in both Amish and non-Amish markets, the appeal of his products and business transcends cultural bounds. The Amishman's story is based on service, innovation, and quality. Abram includes customers in the innovation process and farms out development-stage products to selected users for testing and feedback, a process which also "creates buzz," as he puts it.

"If we can get someone to test our equipment, and they can feel like they're an important part of developing this, that makes people feel good," says Abram. "And if they want to buy something, they're gonna buy this one, because they helped make it." Abram invests both in developing new products and in the tools that help him maintain market position—for example, a recent revamping of the company catalog.

Another heavyweight, Glen Beechy, admits that even a few years ago, he paid little attention to marketing. With a recent slowdown, however, he had to take an interest in order to maintain his leading position in the industry. "I've spent big money the past three years marketing. Big money," he concedes.

Glen sells primarily to wholesale dealers. In the previous year, he set a personal sales record in what was generally considered a down period for the industry. He credits a lot of his recent success to ramped-up marketing.

The difference between advertising and marketing, according to Glen? "If you advertise, you just tell people it's out there. I can run a newspaper ad, but I never know—that's advertising," Glen explains. "But marketing is following up, talking to customers, [asking] 'What can we do?'

"If I send my literature out to a new customer ... I don't just let him look at the literature—there's follow-up phone calls. That's marketing your product, and yourself," Glen says, pointing out the importance of promoting your person, not just the goods or services you provide.

Glen's approach extends the relationship by adding value in different ways. Glen provides in-house employee training for his retailers. He's currently producing a formal sales training program. He'll be able to either sell the program or make it a bonus for top wholesale customers—a unique value-add that few if any competitors offer.

Little extras in his service as well as in the furniture itself make Glen stand out in a crowded field. Hearing him talk about his customer focus, it's no surprise to learn that during one period he expanded each year for six years straight.

Glen's marketing is systematic and organized. He pinpoints his efforts to where they have largest potential impact. He pays close attention to detail. Advertising allows him to initiate a relationship. And he follows up, underscoring the fact that marketing is as much a process of relationship-building as anything else. Perhaps most importantly, the key elements of his story—quality and craftsmanship—are backed up by the products themselves.

MARKETING YOUR MESSAGE: A RECIPE

One straightforward marketing recipe employed to great effect by numerous Amish and non-Amish companies: first pinpoint, create, or boil down a compelling story. Understand your business's appeal, the story you can tell that your competition cannot. If you don't know it, then taking a hard look or asking for outside input can help you identify or develop unique elements within your business. Story in hand, act to promote and further it.

This may mean taking direct action. A story may also emerge organically, with buzz building among satisfied customers. Great stories of course perpetuate themselves. Quality—in products and service—did not become a cliché for no reason.

Some things cannot be faked. As Seth Godin makes clear, marketing a story with little or no basis in reality is a ticket to failure. Consumers are too smart, too well-informed, and have too many choices for inauthentic stories to succeed over any substantial period of time.

Finally, keep in mind that a marketing plan is not something that you hammer someone over the head with. All promotional actions, such as ad campaigns, value-adds, catalogs, and follow-ups, should be considered but steps in a relationship-building process.

People get enough paper and spam thrown at them to instinctively filter most out. Your message will likely be treated the same, unless you can somehow differentiate yourself by inserting a personal element in the process—personal attention in response to action taken by the consumer, for example. Each step in your marketing should be moving you in the direction of a relationship.

How to know when the marketing's working? The benchmark is a customer who is so sold on you—because you did what you promised you would, you did *more* than you promised you would, or something about your business or product simply moved him—that he essentially promotes your business for you.

Top Amish businesses enjoy this type of relationship with their customers and reap the results of their customers' efforts on their behalf. And that can be a lot of fun. We'll take a closer look at conscious steps you can take to enhance word-of-mouth business in the next chapter.

Effective marketing makes sales happen more easily. Yet for many, sales is thought of, at best, a necessary evil. Next, we examine how Amish reap the gains of marketing through effective—even enjoyable—sales, as they take into account both tangible results and the good of the customer.

THE "AMISH MIRACLE HEATER"

The year 2007 saw the grand arrival of a puzzling product on the American consumer scene. Soon after, Amish-looking faces began showing up on late-night infomercials and in full-page ads in publications such as *USA Today, Newsweek,* and *National Geographic,* hawking a wood-encased "miracle heater."

The massive campaign by the Canton, Ohio-based company Heat Surge (with over $40 million spent on advertising in 2008 alone), the two-per-household limit, peculiar regional calling schedule, and especially the prominent connection made with the Amish, all caused more than a few raised eyebrows.

The national scope of the campaign as well as the suspect quality of some of the ads (including one controversial shot of the heater, accompanied by a pair of scantily clad women and a bucket of champagne, appearing in *Rolling Stone* magazine) led many to conclude that the Amish name was being kidnapped yet again.

The Heat Surge company, owned and operated by non-Amish, had in fact arranged for Amish producers to provide the wooden mantelpiece, which housed the "miracle heater" component, allegedly an inexpensive import. Consumers paying the $300 price tag were essentially forking out for the Amish-crafted wood.

The heater has been controversial in Amish communities, with concerns over damage to the Amish reputation as well as high-profile use of the Amish name. At the same time, the degree of involvement on the part of the Amish has apparently been limited. One local source explains that "Amish have never had a hand in the development and promotion of the fireplace—only made the parts." The question remains as to what degree Amish producers are aware of marketing methods used—and based on some of the content, such as the *Rolling Stone* ad, one would guess knowledge has been limited.

As the most prominent use of the Amish name in a marketing context to date, the "miracle heater" example shows the power of the Amish association, even when harnessed and used in ways which would be considered highly "un-Amish" by the Amish themselves.

SALES

Third-grade candy bar campaigns. Jimbo's used-car lot. The life insurance guy.

Sales can be a pain.

Whether you're on the doing end or the receiving end, there are different, often deeply felt reasons to loathe the activity. Much of the ugh factor attached to this linchpin of commerce springs from long-held perceptions of both salespeople and the trade itself.

Everyone has had a bad encounter at some point with a sales "professional" who was anything but. Some were less than ethical. Others may have used pressure and other unsavory tactics to get to yes. When doing the selling ourselves, we feel uncomfortable closing a deal, approaching unreceptive prospects, or facing objections. But unpleasant experiences do not make sales itself a bad thing. And in a consumer world, sales is a fact of life.

Sales goes on around us all the time—in both financial and non-financial situations. Besides everyday purchases, the average person is involved in nonmonetary selling the whole day through. Convincing a friend to attend a Saturday matinee, getting a stubborn child to swallow a forkful of asparagus, or even something as consequential as selling qualifications to an interviewer or loan officer are all examples of day-to-day "nonsales" selling. The brass-tacks truth is that we're all salespeople. Learning to do it well can bring benefits that extend beyond the business arena.

When selling, common rules apply. People respond to authenticity. Humans like to be treated humanely. And no one likes to be run roughshod over. Better to win the day with softer tactics, or not at all. Ultimately, respect for the prospect, manifested in honoring both her time and opinion—along with a willingness to accept a no—are two key elements of effective low-pressure sales.

Sales is the end goal of marketing. Without sales, a business is dead. It may not look dead today, but the day of reckoning will surely come. This is one reason top salespeople are paid so well.

The subdued Amish may not spring immediately to mind when considering the field of sales. Yet some Amish are skilled and experienced salespeople, plying their trade based in a genuine respect for the customer. Ivan Miller is one of them.

SIGNING THEM UP

With a current total of around five hundred customers scattered across the country, Ivan Miller has some experience when it comes to the selling profession.

"I don't try to sell somebody that [doesn't need] my product," Ivan explains, eyes alight beneath a sweaty brow during an afternoon break in harvesting corn. "When I go in to sell, I don't spend days and days on one customer before I ask them, 'How are my prices?' "

Respect in sales means respecting clients' time. And your own. Ivan takes the direct approach for this very reason. Sales is just another area where communication is key.

"I believe in asking questions. Some people might disagree with that, because they say I'm talking all the time." Ivan—rarely at a loss for words—chuckles self-knowingly. "But the more questions you ask them, the more you know where they're coming from."

Ivan's focus on understanding reveals a core customer philosophy. "We want people to be our customers because they *want* to be—that way they'll stick with us."

A crucial part of customers sticking around, Ivan knows, lies in how sales is done. The client's experience matters. Ivan relies on repeat sales. He knows he survives on the strength of his relationships.

This obliges Ivan to streamline the sales process. "I've been in sales . . . close to twenty years now," he recounts. "Where I used to do a three-, four-hour presentation, I could probably do it in one hour now and get a lot more done than I did.

"People don't want to know everything. They want to know, Is it worth my money and time, and is it really a good product? If it is, and I need it, I want it! End of statement."

Outgoing Ivan may seem odd in buttoned-up Amish society. But Amish of differing personalities do sales, just like their English counterparts. It's a learned skill like any other.

The Amishman clearly enjoys it. But he admits it can be tough. "Some people think a salesman doesn't work," Ivan says. "They don't know how that sweat feels."

DIALOGUE, NOT MONOLOGUE

Beginning salespeople, however, find out how that sweat feels, and usually pretty quickly.

Rookie sellers, jittery and leaning on little but a freshly memorized script, often hit hapless early victims—that is, early *prospects*—with a rocket-launcher monologue. While knowing a sales talk is a good foundation and confidence-booster, as a rule, better results come from genuine dialogue.

Pennsylvania barn builder Eli King feels sales is best done live. "I try to make a point of meeting every customer . . . at least before I hand them a bid," he explains. Face-to-face, Eli maintains, is the best way to make a good first impression.

Mild-mannered and soft-spoken, Eli is in many ways the exact opposite of Ivan Miller. One customer, Eli explains, first checked out a few of his competitors. "He said I was the first one to actually come out and meet with him. And to me that meant a lot"—but more importantly—"to *him* that meant a lot."

Eli continues the personal approach through the entire process. "From the beginning, I like to ask the customer a lot of questions," he explains, a practice shared with Ivan Miller. A customer compared Eli's inquisitive approach to that of competitors. Where others ask two or three questions, Eli goes through fifteen or twenty.

"He liked that. Because we're trying to find out what he needs."

Asking questions works in three ways: by eliciting useful information, by conveying genuine concern on a "real person" level, and finally, in exuding a professionalism that helps prospects have confidence. Potential customers want to feel listened to, they want to feel like you care, and they want to feel secure in you as someone to whom they might be entrusting large sums of money. Thoughtful, personalized, pinpointed questions can address all three issues.

READING THE SIGNS AND LOVING THE NOS

When talking shop, die-hard salespeople often review "buying signs," verbal and nonverbal signals that indicate whether a given prospect is likely to buy or not.

Buying signs can range from the crossed-arms-and-grunts stance to the customer who lights a cigarette or offers a refreshment at the close. Some place full faith in buying signs; others see them as less reliable.

Eli King explains that "some customers, they'll look at it, they'll nod their head—you can tell by their reaction you've got your finger in the deal.

"Then there's some where you think you've got them, but then they're gone." Though buying signs may deceive at times, there is value in learning to discern interest.

For that matter, salespeople should recognize that a customer is not always "closeable" after one meeting, depending on the specific selling situation. Some require time to ponder, a point which becomes truer as the size of the sale increases.

Thus the importance of an open-door policy when first attempts come up short. "I don't like pushing them. I don't like handing them a bid," Eli explains, "and give 'em a minute to look at it, [then] say, 'Are you gonna buy this?'" The Amishman cracks up, amused at the bluntness of the unfortunately typical rookie closing question. As anyone who's tried it knows, well-do-you-want-it? is a surefire way to crank up the pressure.

Eli gets back in touch if he hasn't gotten a response in a week or two. Using unassumptive wording, he informs prospects that "I don't want to pressure you, but that I just want to know sort of what's ahead of me so I can schedule and plan ahead," he explains. "Usually they appreciate that. They thank you for calling."

Eli recognizes that some of his prospects may not be ready to buy today. But he knows that the situation may be different in six months or a year's time.

The end goal? A yes—*or* a no. Both are positive in that they allow him to move on and concentrate resources of time, money, and energy elsewhere, and move toward tangible results.

People love to buy but hate to be sold. It's a hard and fast truth. The average shopper, for instance, shuns unsolicited assistance as if it came not from a pimply teenager but a plague-stricken space mutant.

"Buzz off," we feel the urge to say, faced with an interruption of our leisurely browsing.

Respecting a prospect's space—and conveying the absolute acceptability of a negative response—brings a sale a lot closer than pressure and pushiness.

If you really don't care whether a given prospect buys, he becomes more comfortable—and more likely to do so. But low-pressure salespeople face a dilemma: the necessity of doing your absolute best presentation but with a detached interest that views refusal as a perfectly acceptable outcome.

Focusing on quantity reduces pressure. More sales calls to more prospects means more sales. A numbers commitment relieves pressure from individual sales situations.

Counterintuitively, nos are in fact acceptable. It's the maybes, those that stretch long term while sucking up time and emotional energy, that are the real killers. Learning to ascertain true interest and when to cut losses lessens the heartache that "maybe" brings.

But often, assuming the signs are there, patience can be a virtue. "Usually when you hear back from them, it's a good sign," explains Eli. "They've had a chance to look at other companies, and they must have liked something about your bid."

There comes a time to close. But in some cases it's important to leave prospects feeling it's alright to say yes later. Eli's approach reveals the value of patience.

Some fields, especially those involving smaller sales, may require more immediate decisions. But discerning interest, being comfortable with a no—or even *inviting* one—as well as understanding that not all prospects will buy today are all key elements of effective low-pressure sales.

Mastering these elements can reduce stress, increase both sales and the amount of work time spent productively, and make the selling side of business a lot more enjoyable.

Persistence is often cited as a key to sales success. When selling, Ivan Miller is direct and perseverant. Eli King is more reserved and patient.

Elam Peachey is still working through the question of how persistent to be.

"Do I call once a month, once a week, every day?" Elam asks. "What is pleasant persistence? Where do you become annoying?"

Answering his own question, Elam says that "it depends on the customer, I think." Some react positively. Others less so. "Pleasant persistence" is a hallmark of many successful salespeople but can be hard for some to become comfortable with. Identifying when you have become annoying is more art than science.

When you persist in a spirit of respect and genuine conviction that your product or service will improve your clients' situation, they sense your authenticity and are more likely to respond favorably. You'll feel better about yourself as well. Persistence that springs from focusing solely on your personal bank account is another matter.

The degree to which a person "pleasantly persists" often depends on personality. Unsurprisingly, best results usually come when the style of selling fits the person doing the selling.

VISUALIZING THE SALE

In the sales process, price presentation is a separate element worth special attention. Keeping our metaphors rural, the price can be a bit like a pig: it usually needs some dressing up before you want to kiss it.

According to Dennis Miller, delivering the price is "a major part" of the sales process.

The nature of his industry and the size of the jobs make sitting down and explaining why things cost what they do a must. "If you don't, if you just send it to them in the mail—I've done that—you hardly ever get that customer."

Often, the price doesn't affect the final decision as much as the presentation does. "If you can do a super presentation, that $5,000 might not mean anything," Dennis explains, citing "details and information" as key elements of a good presentation.

Dennis invests a few dollars per prospect to create a personalized binder that includes his company's literature. Potential clients are left with a professional-looking document holder in which to place all relevant paperwork over the course of the (at this point still hypothetical) project.

Dennis presents the binder as part of his initial pitch, leaving prospects with a small taste of the experience of working with him. It's a brilliant way to plant the seed that he'd be a professional, competent person to employ. Dennis's binder is subtly assumptive, but not "in your face" enough to turn off more timid prospects.

In various ways, including through thoughtful questions, you can help clients visualize hiring you or purchasing your product. Real estate agents, for example, use staging techniques to spruce up a home's visual appeal, and ask theoretical "would" questions, as in "How would you use this room?"

One Amish cabinetmaker trots out three-dimensional artist-drawn diagrams to help potential clients picture their future kitchens. The visual aid "blows them away most times," he says, claiming the diagrams alone have sold numerous jobs.

Helping prospects visualize the sale can be the decisive step as you close. Little extras like Dennis's client binder and professionally produced company literature are tiny investments that can potentially pay for themselves many thousandfold.

Amish may be frugal, but helping clients visualize the sale is one area where Dennis and others do not skimp. Don't shun small expenditures that can help make big sales.

CLOSING IT DOWN

Through all the sweat, Ivan Miller has laser-honed his sales presentation, becoming much more efficient and effective, saving himself and prospects valuable time.

Well-executed sales, as with many other things in the well-run Amish firm, comes down to simplicity. "In general, we make life way too hard," Ivan observes. "Keep it basic, ask the questions, and move on. Ask for the sale!"

Effective closing means being assumptive. "It's like, when somebody's standing there looking, I ask them, 'So how many do you want?'" Rather than, he adds, adopting a comical voice, "I don't mean to bug you, but are you interested?"

Beginners often squirm at this step in the cycle. But closing assertively is in a certain sense doing a service. It means bringing a presentation to a timely conclusion as well as giving the other side an opportunity to ask questions and voice concerns.

But the salesperson needs to stay aware of the climate in the room. Putting people on the spot—by bumping pressure up too quickly, for example—usually results in procrastination or a variety of other creative reasons for not buying today.

Though Ivan and others are assumptive, objections and questions need to be answered before progress can be made. Some salespeople prefer a series of questions that ask for smaller commitments rather than the full sale all at once. "Yes or no?" can be off-putting.

Ivan may seem forward. Yet the Amishman tempers his approach with humility. "I've been reminded many a time, God gives different gifts, and it's not always as easy for some people as others. I realize that," he concedes. "But oftentimes we make it too hard for ourselves."

BOILING IT DOWN

Sales done effectively—and based in humility and respect—can be boiled down to a few key points.

Ask lots of questions. Be well enough informed to be able to answer prospects' questions—and then some. Get comfortable with the idea of "no" and convey that acceptance.

Follow up, but persist in a good-natured manner. Use visuals, questions, and face-to-face contact to help prospects envision bringing their business to you. When the time comes to close, do so with confidence. And if after answering questions and objections you get a decisive no, be happy with it—"no" being a response worlds better than the dreaded, dragging "maybe."

Following these ideas means treating a potential customer with respect. You'll also communicate that dealing with you is different from what she's probably used to.

Sales is something every businessperson must do at some point, be it products to customers, ideas to employees, or oneself to a bank, board, or potential partner.

Sales can be fun when done right. Done in a spirit of respect and with an eye to building a long-term bond—rather than extracting short-term personal gain—sales becomes both financially rewarding and personally fulfilling.

Sales respectfully done is key to forging and furthering productive customer relationships. The customer relationship is in many cases the foundation of Amish and non-Amish firms' success. In the next chapter, we'll examine that relationship against the backdrop of generating word-of-mouth business. We'll also look at situations in which *not* pursuing a relationship with a given person may actually turn out to be in your best interest.

NINE POINTS ON SALES AND MARKETING

1. Marketing won't solve the fundamental problem of a subpar product.

2. A business's unique story can form the basis of its marketing approach. Developing or uncovering your story may take work but brings rewards.

3. Marketing is relationship-building. Those who follow up with a personalized response get noticed.

4. Marketing is a process, whereas advertising is a onetime event. Advertising can comprise a core element of a marketing strategy, but advertising alone is not a marketing strategy.

5. In sales situations, people want to be treated like people. This means questions, dialogue, listening, and an openness to nos. Professionals treat prospects like people, not tools.

6. Conviction in your product, business, or service makes it easier to pleasantly persist.

7. Visual aids, open-ended questions, and presenting in person can all help close sales.

8. Numbers relieve pressure. Knowing you have five, fifteen, or fifty more prospects to see makes the result of any individual sales call diminish greatly in importance.

9. Sales is made easier by well-executed marketing. Sales done in a spirit of respect can be fulfilling and profitable.

CHAPTER FOUR

DOING UNTO OTHERS

The Crucial Customer Relationship

Quality's why we're busy.
Price just doesn't matter a whole lot—if they know you're really good.
—AMISH STONEWORKER

M enno Graber apparently sees parallels between the people who buy his chairs and the Pope in Rome. "The customer's always right," he proclaims, "even if he's wrong."

Customer infallibility is just one of the business riddles Menno has spent the morning deciphering as we sit in his modest office.

Somehow, I realize only later, I've commandeered the ultra-comfy executive rocker, while Menno—company boss, local bishop, and thirty-five years my senior—perches across the desk on the wooden seat where itinerant sales guys usually sit.

Menno never acknowledges my error, carrying on without a word. It's a slow Saturday, and maybe he's having too much fun. "You know, you get a customer mad. . . . You can't tell him off," Menno adds. "You just have to go with it."

True, you can't exactly tell him off. Though yes, even Amish sometimes feel like blasting the occasional irritating customer. Or the one that avoids you like swine flu when billing time comes around.

"We got a lot of good customers," Menno says, explaining the flexible approach he takes to accounts receivable. At the same time, he says, some delinquent accounts simply don't answer their phones. So, demonstrating a bit of Amish tech savvy, Menno takes advantage of his phone's "star-67" feature to smokescreen calls.

Customers can be a source of frustration. At the same time, Amish know who is paying the bills. Amish managers stress keeping the customer happy. And in practice this means a lot more than the occasional pleasantry.

"Our biggest competitive edge is our relationship with our customers," one entrepreneur explains. "My competition can't take that away from us," he declares, calling it a "personal, emotional" connection. "I'd rather have that than be the cheapest."

Bad experiences can be powerful, and negative word of mouth can quickly dismantle a hard-built reputation. As one veteran puts it, "You can treat ten customers good, but nobody'll find it out; but if you treat one customer bad, one hundred people will find it out."

Why do bad stories spread more quickly than the good ones? Negative people, by virtue of feeling slighted, are a lot more motivated to talk—and more loudly. Chalk it up to human nature.

The point, then, is to avoid creating negative people while pumping out armies of contented clients. In this chapter, we'll examine ways Amish business owners do just that—by taking proactive steps to keep customers happy, by assuring quality and service, by absorbing and quelling frustration and dissatisfaction on the infrequent occasions they experience it.

We'll also take a look at the best course of action when things don't work out. Stay in business long enough and you'll meet the customer you wish you'd never laid eyes on. The walking migraine, why-couldn't-you-have-called-my-competitor hopeless case.

No matter what you do, he's not happy. In fact, he won't ever be. And nothing you do will change that. "Sometimes it's not just about the job," explains one Amishman, "it's because of all the baggage that he brought with him."

Even if Mr. Nasty helps the bottom line, you've sacrificed far more than he was worth in time, stress, pride, or other limited resources. As a means of defense, some take no-nonsense action by tactfully not accepting resource-draining customers in the first place.

In the following look at the customer, we'll take stock of how Amish create and foster relationships with satisfied customers, the ultimate catalyst for word-of-mouth business.

We'll look at the reasoning behind *why* businesses ought to do the things everyone already knows intuitively—like deliver quality and customer service—by examining these elements in the context of generating future business.

Finally, we'll peer into the dark side to explore how Amish handle both problem customers and customer problems, and we'll extract the philosophies which undergird a compassionate yet results-oriented approach to challenging situations.

But first, a closer look at the truism.

THE TRUTH IN THE TRUISM

As worn as the adage may be, Amish acknowledge that the customer holds the reins. Entrepreneurs in the community live and breathe this wisdom. Customer focus even finds its way into the business vision. "I had a vision and a business philosophy," recounts Glen Beechy. "You take care of your customer, and the customer's always right."

Glen's customers are sold on him. And it's easy to see why. "Interacting [with customers is] big time," says Glen. Customer service pays, particularly on the top end. And Glen realizes how it benefits the bottom line. He knows sales figures and who his heaviest-hitting customers are, information he uses to funnel resources where they can have greatest impact.

Pennsylvania metal worker Mervin Riehl is resigned to the truism. But he realizes it can still be a challenge. "The customer is not always right, but he's always the customer," he explains. "If he says this is the way he wants it, then make it the way he wants it.

"You would hope that the customer would let you know that he's not totally satisfied," Mervin says, "and then you have to fix it, make it over, do whatever it takes, until the customer is satisfied. If you don't, he's not your customer," Mervin says. "That's just the bottom line. He'll go somewhere else.

"If there is mistakes, that's one thing," the Amishman points out. "But it's what you do about the mistakes that you make is what really is gonna tell in the long run."

SPOKES IN THE WHEEL

What you do about those mistakes is a critical spoke in the customer-business relationship. Service, along with other spokes of the customer experience, is crucial in developing loyalty, and ultimately in gearing up a powerful word-of-mouth machine. Spokes of the relationship include

- Service
- The Golden Rule
- Quality
- Effective, relevant communication
- Managing customer expectations and perception of your business

Each can either strengthen or weaken the relationship with a given customer. Everyone knows that these Customer 101 principles are important. We don't often spend much time reflecting on why. Besides the good feelings that come from operating a business with integrity, what tangible benefits do they bring?

Deal done, a customer can take one or more of four actions in the future: (1) do business with you again; (2) recommend you to others; (3) choose not to do business with you again; (4) advise others *against* doing business with you (or worse). Excelling at these elements means managing toward the desired outcomes of (1) and (2), and preventing (4) in particular.

Many Amish take satisfaction from pleasing customers through exceptional services and products. It's the right thing to do.

But they also know to manage current customers with the goal of gaining new ones in the future. The end goal is not just contentment but also the tangible gains found in (1) and (2). This happens when businesses get the five spokes right.

Starting with customer service, we'll examine each spoke and how it feeds into word of mouth and repeat business. A customer will recommend you or come back for more only if she is pleased with the work you've done, and trusts you. What follows is a breakdown of how the Amish achieve those two things.

HEAR ME SMILE

Customer service comprises multiple elements. Good customer service includes solving problems—ones you've created and ones you didn't. It's also courtesy. It means making the customer feel he's the most important person in the room. And these elements have greatest impact when done in the context of building a bond over time.

"We try to build a relationship, rather than just a customer.... That's just so important," says Abram Gingerich, the nation's top manufacturer in his specialty field. "Because when he needs something, he'll buy it from you." Abram realizes that solid relationships are largely a factor of time and consistent behavior. You build integrity when you keep your promises, follow up, and resolve problems promptly.

At its most basic level, explains a leather artisan, "you have to have an interest in the people.... They'll realize that very quick if ... you just want to sell them a product and get their money, then shove them out the door. They can feel that when they come in," he warns.

A bicycle shop owner counsels against taking customers for granted. "That's sometimes easy to do," he admits. "You have these regular customers, then once in a while, you'll see, 'Oh, they bought a bike somewhere else.' You wonder why."

A furniture maker fixes problems as an "ongoing service," even those he didn't cause, in order to "keep them on our side." Maintenance with hardwood furniture is a real issue, he explains, pointing out that "wood never dies," which means continuous expansion and contraction.

"Once they know that you'll take care of [them], then they'll trust you, and they're willing to try your new products too." This owner has pinpointed a service issue and has focused his customer service approach around solving an industry-wide problem.

Amish communities often have at least one Coleman dealer. The lamps, often accepted as a form of lighting, are popular among Amish. Over a century ago, company founder William Coffin Coleman showed how customer service can overcome the lack of trust sowed by the ill dealings of others, while laying the foundations for his ubiquitous firm by focusing on customer satisfaction.

Selling in the town of Kingfisher, Oklahoma, Coleman happened upon unhappy customers feeling bilked by a previous salesman whose products had quickly become clogged with carbon deposits and could not be cleaned. In order to overcome the trust deficit left behind by the previous dealer, Coleman leased his lamps for $1 a week instead of selling them. He also serviced the lamps himself. If they proved faulty, customers were not charged. Coleman's personal approach to service was a hit; his product's quality proved itself; sales ballooned; and Coleman is a household name today. Coleman, along with many Amish today, recognized the value of creating trust through impeccable customer service.

SQUEAKY WHEELS

Amishman Dennis Miller does remodeling work. Some jobs run into the hundreds of thousands of dollars. Dennis may work with a given client for up to a year, and have as many as twelve projects in process at any given time.

Providing consistent, blue-ribbon service to multiple customers, Dennis says, can be challenging. "The wheel that squeaks the loudest is the one that gets oiled."

Over twenty years in the industry, most as an owner, Dennis has become adept at communicating and managing expectations. "You have to make each and every customer feel they are the most important customer out there—regardless [of whether] you want to or not.

"You can't tell them, 'I'm sorry I didn't show up yesterday, because I was over at so-and-so's job,'" Dennis warns, "because in a sense you're telling them, 'Well, he was more important than ... you are.'"

Alvin Hershberger makes an interesting comparison with his employee relationship. "Even though my employees are on a higher level than my customers, we make the customer feel that they are.

"My employees mean more to me, because I see them everyday," he continues. "But, I tell them that if I'm not here, and that customer comes, you go and [serve] that customer. Don't make him wait more than five minutes. Because we have a reputation."

Alvin's focus is repetitive and comprehensive. It's not just a dab of politeness while the client reaches for his wallet. He strives to create an across-the-board positive experience, from the retail floor to the manufacturing shop to the loading dock, so that customers make consistently positive associations wherever they may find themselves. Alvin's business revolves around a specific narrative, and his service is a key element of that story.

Alvin knows that reputation spreads, and that there is no limit to the channels through which it can be advanced. The relationship is not just with the person paying the invoice. It's with any and all involved.

Crucially, the strength of any relationship is tested not when things are going well but when problems, stress, and crises arise. Amish business owners like Alvin are adamant about making mistakes right. They work to make sure customers walk out the door happy. They recognize they are going to win their customers' hearts in these moments, and they step up when difficulties arise.

Says one Amish entrepreneur, "Our customers know that they can ask any question they want. Because they can feel that they are our number one source of income," he explains. "They know that we know that they could fire us."

But once trust is established—and so long as it is maintained—the bond formed can be incredible. "Once they trust you," explains this veteran, "you can basically stand there and write orders."

GOLDEN RULE

Underlying the idea of customer service is the concept of brotherly good. Considering how the average Amish businessperson's life meshes with business, it's no surprise to see the Golden Rule at play both in the day-to-day and in the shop.

Bishop Menno Graber offers his two cents on doing the right thing. "The more you put in, the more you get out," he explains.

"It's like anything else. You can't get interest at the bank if you don't put no money in! It's just like charity. But you don't have to go and tell a fellow that I donated so much money for this.

"If anything happens, we repair free," says Menno, noting that he honors this guarantee on issues that appear even ten years after purchase, which has happened on occasion. Retailers can return product on discovering any problems. The guarantee even extends to the retail customer. Menno's promise reflects confidence in his chairs' craftsmanship (though there are limits: "dogs chewing legs off," to the disappointment of some, is not covered).

Taking on service obligations means incurring greater costs but gives the buyer the assurance of satisfaction. That certainty can tip a person in one direction when considering where to take his dollars. True, servicing old stuff eats up time that could be spent producing new stuff. But it helps build a reputation, leading to sales down the line.

Menno focuses on preventing defective merchandise ever leaving the shop. Though denying perfection, he claims steady improvement.

"I always tell my workers," Menno pauses, "never send anything out there that you wouldn't want yourself."

Menno's message resonates with many Amish. Recall the Sunday sermon story of the deceptive carpenter. Contracted by his brother to build a house, he cuts corners and uses subpar materials. The other guy is going to get stuck with it, but how will he know?

Then the generous sibling turns the tables. "The home you have built is for you, my brother." In the end, he had only stuck himself.

Menno likely knows the story by heart. He may even have preached it on Sunday. "Some people [think], 'Well, this won't hurt, they won't see it.'...Well, then, if you buy it, would you want it that way?"

QUALITY

"Quality of the furniture is excellent"; "workmanship was outstanding"; "exemplary" attention to details; "well-crafted, solid." Judging by these and other customer comments, many have a remarkably positive impression of Amish goods. In one Penn State study, nearly all respondents perceived Amish products to be of higher quality than corresponding non-Amish ones.

Quality is a running narrative in Amish business circles. Amish firms tend to compete on quality and service before price. "Add a buck and you can get by with it," says one woodworker. "But if you do bad work, you're not around long."

Producing good quality, and knowing it, empowers a business owner. Quality can mean being able to charge more. Amish-produced products and services are not necessarily the most expensive, but they are also typically not the cheapest. Plenty pay for what they perceive to be—and in many cases actually is—higher-than-average quality.

As many high-flying firms have discovered, quality can fall by the wayside during boom times. How to maintain it, especially when growing?

Jason Glick, who has recently tripled his employee roster, admits that quality "was an issue. It probably still is some. But I'm very fortunate to have some lead guys that are just crazy [about] quality."

Having employees that are nuts about work well done is one thing. But it has to come from somewhere. Jason drives it.

Quality is a common focus at Jason's biannual meetings. Getting employees to buy in takes a strong example. "When I come out on a job and see something's not right, I make them change it," he says. "I think that helps too, that they know that I *am* going to stop in there," Jason suggests, "that they can't get away with it."

The boss sets the tone. "I just keep pumping that into their heads all the time ... quality's why we're busy." Some will take initiative themselves. Others need monitoring.

When it comes to getting employees to do quality work, "I really beat them up on that," says one Amishman, using an odd choice of words for a member of a pacifist religious group. "Be a light," he adds, saying he doesn't care how fast a job is done as long as it's done properly.

Glen Beechy has succeeded at preserving quality during many periods of growth. "And that wasn't just me. That was my employees. I put people in place to control the quality. And I tell you what, we were right on. Our quality was controlled." Glen claims hearing positive comments on his ability to maintain quality "over and over and over."

His quality focus has yielded concrete results, even though he faced criticism from certain parties for his customer-centric approach. Despite the skeptics, "I gained the confidence of my customers," Glen explains, smiling. *"They don't go anywhere."*

INTERCOURSE AND THE "UNDER-OVER" BALANCE

The quaint hamlet of Intercourse lies in the heart of the Lancaster settlement. Home to numerous Amish, Intercourse is a popular destination for Plain-curious urbanites. The oddly named village also provides the punch line for many a joke made by out-of-towners, stamped on tourist trinkets, and originating from local Amish themselves.

As it happens, intercourse is also crucial to the Amish firm. Amish businesspeople emphasize frequent, meaningful intercourse with their customers as one secret to their success. But before this book gets tossed in the trash, let's back up and revisit the word's original meaning. Yes, there was a time when "intercourse" had nothing to do with making babies—a definition first recorded at the turn of the nineteenth century—and everything to do with *communication*.

Lancaster Amishman Elam Peachey relates how important communication is in his business. And especially in managing expectations.

"I believe in the under-promise/over-deliver aspect, but if you under-promise to the point where you say it's going to take eight weeks to build a deck, they're going to say, 'This guy's nuts.' " Elam emphasizes, "You need to make sure you're realistic with your promising, but then try to [finish] inside of that.

"The biggest thing there, again, is communication." If you find you've budgeted too little time for a job, for example, it's important to be up front about it. In such situations, "you didn't necessarily meet their expectations. But if you handle it properly, they won't mind." Preemptive action makes the difference.

The point is to strike a balance between reality and customer expectations—between under-promising and over-delivering—and then manage those expectations. And if you happen to err, then confront the issue quickly with the goal of finding an acceptable solution.

Communication can take various forms. Communication may mean daily, weekly, monthly, quarterly, or yearly contact. It may mean face-to-face interaction or the occasional e-mail. It may be formal presentations or a casual drop-in while in the neighborhood. It may require visual aides for visual people, or it may involve reviewing what was agreed in a previous meeting. However it's done, tailored communication eliminates headaches and furthers the relationship.

Ezra Miller believes in dynamic interaction with clients. He claims that 100 percent of his customers originate from word-of-mouth recommendations. Yet even armed with those recommendations, he still has to sell himself—as reliable and trustworthy—to prospective clients.

To do that, Ezra relies on customer references. Recommendations can be a powerful tool. If clients offer, don't turn them down, and don't be afraid to ask for them.

Communication starts from day zero—before even securing the job. First impressions are by definition one-shot occurrences. To convey respect, Ezra says that "you can't go in and be in a hurry when you meet them. You cater to them."

Communication goes beyond an exchange of ideas or concerns. Ezra fosters communicative relationships by getting customers involved in unconventional ways.

"A lot of homeowners think you're pushing them off if you're telling them the permit's not ready," Ezra explains. "I get my customers involved to *help* get the permit. Sometimes it can be a long [process]." Being involved, they better understand challenges and feel empowered by playing a role in the ultimate success of the project.

Manage expectations. Customers need to hear from you about progress, or about why it's not occurring. Convey trustworthiness through evidence, such as references, and genuine personal interaction. And involve them in the job if possible.

THE DOUBLE-EDGED DRAW OF TOURISM

The "peculiar people" have a peculiar relationship with the tourist industry.

Ground zero for Amish tourism, Lancaster County, gets hardest hit thanks to a longstanding tourist orientation coupled with its close proximity to major East Coast urban centers. An estimated ten million visitors make the trek to the historic county yearly. The Amish are without doubt the top draw.

Tourist industries are also well developed in other large Amish settlements, such as Holmes County and northern Indiana, and present in numerous other communities from Iowa to upstate New York.

Tourism both benefits and irritates Amish. On the plus side, local economies enjoy the boon of tourist money. Out-of-towners patronize tourist-oriented businesses and also purchase furniture and other goods the Amish produce. Outside attention can have a reinforcing cultural effect, reminding the Amish of defining differences and helping to solidify a sense of identity.

On the other hand, Amish usually aren't too keen on camera-wielding interlopers. Tourists also add to road traffic, already considerable in some areas due to growing non-Amish populations. Amish generally try to be accommodating and responsive to genuine-hearted interest in their way of life, yet they dislike zoo-exhibit treatment.

The 1985 release of the murder drama *Witness,* set in Lancaster County and starring a roster of big-name actors, was a watershed for Amish tourism, ratcheting up an already existent industry. Media coverage, a torrent of Amish-themed fiction, and a steady stream of television and documentaries have also kept the Plain People present in the American consciousness and their communities planted firmly on the list of domestic vacation hotspots.

Tourism is a double-edged sword, and it shows few signs of subsiding as both Amish population as well as the Plain presence in pop culture continue to expand.

WORD OF MOUTH: MANAGING FOR THE NEXT JOB

Numerous Amish in diverse industries rely heavily on word of mouth to generate new business. And success in getting word-of-mouth business is built on everything we've covered so far: quality, effective communication, the Golden Rule, and so on.

Landscaper Mark Miller promotes his business in various venues. But word of mouth he calls, hands-down, "the best advertising." When happy customers tell neighbors about you, there's "just so much more chance that you can get the job."

Results, of course, vary. But a focus on word of mouth, applied consistently over time, reaps real benefits. "Some people, you don't get anybody, but the next person, you'll get relatives, neighbors, friends," Mark points out. "You'll get five or six jobs off of one person. And that's incredible."

Amish business owners recognize the potential implications of each job. Sometimes this necessitates sacrifices of both pride and money. "We've had a few that we had some problems with," Mark explains, "and we'll lose money just to keep them happy."

An issue arose at one newly built home, unrelated to the work Mark's company had performed. Even though the problem was pre-existing, in such cases, "we'll always go back and fix it."

Going out of your way or even going in the hole, especially when you're not the one at fault, is no fun. But, Mark feels, "it's worth it, because of the advertising."

Good service fosters repeat business. Sadie Lapp credits customer satisfaction as a prime reason for repeat purchases of her quilts, noteworthy when the majority of her customers, primarily consisting of tourists, live outside of her home area. How you treat present customers directly influences acquiring future ones as well. Elam Peachey knows this, and proactively bolsters the customer's peace of mind.

Arriving at a jobsite on a gusty day, Elam found scrap metal strewn across the backyard. He quickly gathered the pieces and weighed them down to prevent it happening again. Elam had described this particular customer as a joy to work with, and wanted to avoid any chance of damaging the relationship.

At another job, a few shingles, yet to seal because of cold temperatures, had blown off the home. Elam called the customers to inform them of the problem, explain why it happened, and let them know it was slated to be fixed. Elsewhere, Elam repositioned a fallen-over sign advertising his business. Elam constantly monitors public perception of his firm and the customer's impression of his work.

Little things get noticed. Clunky web design, an untucked shirttail, or an impatient tone of voice all play into a customer's perception of you and your operation, coloring their view of both the business and the work you've done.

Elam manages each job with an eye to the next. He keeps aware that how well he does on his present project can mean the difference between having work and not having it in a few months' time. Customer satisfaction takes on that much more significance when viewed as a driver of future business.

Quality, the Golden Rule, customer service, communication, and management of customer expectations are the spokes in the wheel of customer satisfaction. That wheel can still turn when one is missing, but it's a choppier ride. Aim to get them all right and reap tangible benefits, as Amish do, of word of mouth and repeat business.

THE CUSTOMER-CONSULTANT

Communication, as examined in the last section, is important for the customer's confidence, understanding, and peace of mind. But astute businesspeople realize that the customer can teach them a lot as well. And that it's wise to listen when a customer has something to say—even though it may not always be easy.

Amish often get product ideas from customers. Christian King, who runs a business providing furniture and interior accessories in the heart of Lancaster County, keeps his ear to the ground. "I keep it in the back of my head—this customer asked for this—and if you get two or three more like that, well, maybe I should venture into that."

Christian says that if a number of "main customers" favor a certain product, that knowledge will typically influence what he produces. Top people carry more weight.

Customers can give special insight on the sales process. Eli King recalls one whose input was "worth a hundred bucks." The client provided real-life insight into the market and how Eli's offer stacked up against the competitors'.

"He told me that our price was higher ... and he said he wants to sit down and compare apples to apples," Eli recounts. "He came in my office, and we laid everything out." The experience opened Eli's eyes to where competitors were beating him. It took nerve to sit and listen to why he wasn't good enough. But Eli did.

Seeing your business, product, or service through the customer's eyes reveals strengths and weaknesses. It may be as simple as asking.

It could require a more formal follow-up, such as a survey or feed-back form.

Businesspeople like Eli know that you can learn as much or more from no as from yes. If you find a customer willing to share, bite your lip, nod, and take lots of notes. Unforced, self-motivated comments tend to be more candid and relevant. Managers who put ego aside, pay attention, and absorb the messages customers send benefit by tapping into a potent, highly relevant source of information. Think of it as freebie consulting from the inside out.

PAMPERING YOUR GOLDEN GEESE

Customers come in all shapes and sizes. Which are more important, the big or the small? Bigger ones obviously have greater individual impact on sales. Losing one hurts. But in the long run, today's smaller customer could be just as valuable.

Consistently great service for all should be the goal. But top cus-tomers need something extra. "My top twenty are definitely 80 percent of my business, which, that's the way it always works," explains Glen Beechy.

The 80/20 rule to which Glen refers is the maxim which states that a majority of results—be they sales, headaches, profits—come from a minority of inputs. This is commonly stated as an 80:20 ratio, but it can be more skewed. Those in the top 10 percent income bracket pay over two-thirds of all taxes. Less than 1 percent of the population commits 80 percent of crimes.

The point is that the bulk of a certain output can often be traced to a small body of producers. In business this means taking special care of your top people. "I wine and dine my top twenty," Glen admits. Knowing his numbers helps Glen pinpoint his efforts.

And the implicit other side of the coin: avoid getting bogged down with the low-producing end. According to the 80/20 rule, efforts spent on the high end will return scores more than the same effort fired at the bottom. Low producers simply burn more resources, pound for pound, than large ones. Sometimes much more.

Glen delivers good customer service to everyone, but he's particularly adamant about providing it for the top tier, essentially the drivers of his business.

At the same time, some Amish are cautious about relying too much on a few large accounts. Katie Beiler, a Pennsylvania greenhouse owner, explains how one large client negatively impacted her business, compelling her to tie up limited storage area in order to adapt to the buyer's pick-up schedule. Seeing how this hampered her service to the rest of her customers, she eventually broke ties with the large account to better serve the rest of her business.

Other Amish concur on the potential peril of relying on one or a handful of primary buyers. Discussing another business that allegedly relied on a single buyer for 95 percent of its sales, metal shop owner Mervin Riehl described the case as "95 percent risky," adding, "That'd scare me. I wouldn't want to be in that position.... If something happens and he all of a sudden decides to go somewhere else, well what are these guys gonna do?"

While top customers are important, most Amish sensibly realize the danger of placing too much stock in one or a few clients.

WATERING SEEDS

While it may be true that only a small percentage of your customers cause most of the headaches, what about smaller clients who are perfectly reasonable . . . just maybe too small to bother with?

Though the top end may drive your business today, mighty trees start as tiny seeds. Turning up your nose at mini orders could mean chucking future sales on the trashpile. "You want to be careful what you say no to, because you never know where it could end up at," says one Amishman.

"We don't turn nothing down," says a cabinet shop owner. "It can be from one little door to a $150,000 job." The reason? "It can lead to a big job. . . . We're just kind of afraid that if we get picky, we're gonna get greedy," he admits.

"A lot of times if we . . . take care of a small customer, he remembers that. He's gonna refer other people to us." Larger orders may result. The cabinetmaker says this has happened "a lot of times." The shop even has an individual specially tasked to handle smaller orders.

On small requests, an Ohio Amish entrepreneur says to "have a positive attitude about it, so the customers feel like 'Hey, I'm not bothering him.'" Even if you're not excited, "you can't let that on to the customer. . . . You've got to make it sound like you're happy."

No one wants to feel like they are bothering someone. This entrepreneur has felt exactly that way when patronizing other businesses. "I've ordered stuff where they hee-hawed back and forth, they didn't want to do it; finally they agreed. Well, if I could get somebody else to do it the next time, I was gonna do it."

If it means a multiyear relationship, even the most menial job pays off. The challenge comes in not knowing which time-consuming task will bear fruit. Solve enough problems for enough people, no matter how small, and some will prove themselves worth far more than they seemed at first.

Snap-on Tools is a good example of a company focused on solving customer problems. Snap-on emphasizes flexibility and respect for smaller buyers. Company dealers, catering to automotive specialists, make weekly rounds in their vans, which hold thousands of dollars worth of tools and supplies. Snap-on dealers can be game-savers for an under-the-gun mechanic needing a specialty tool.

Dealers are known to be creative and flexible with financing, collecting trade-ins and weekly payments in an interest-free arrangement that encourages the little guy to participate. Known for the high quality of their tools, Snap-on has also gained the respect of their clientele, celebrated by the company in ads lauding the professionals of the automotive world. Snap-on's flexible, inclusive approach to selling—one that acknowledges the small buyer—has brought the firm the benefit of customer loyalty and made it a leader in its field.

When handling smaller customers, a final PR element is at work too. Refusing someone outright, especially in a tactless manner, sends a terrible message, one which instantly creates an unhappy "customer"—one who's never even officially done business with you but already knows two things from her experience: that she doesn't like you, and that maybe the people in her social and professional circles shouldn't like you either.

"In any distribution business, there's gonna be a few customers that actually cost you money," says one Amishman. "But what it would cost to tell a customer like that that they're disqualified to continue would cost a lot more than what you lose with them by dealing with them."

GETTING AROUND

The grey-topped buggy creeps slowly up the hill, approaching the crest. Suddenly, two dozen leather-clad figures, hunched on Harley hogs, roll up just behind—engines popping—following along at a clip-clop pace. Eventually, the carriage ascends far enough to allow the bikers the sight line needed to pass safely.

For a fleeting moment, an Amishman and his horse led a biker gang through this back corner of Lancaster County, offering a choice shot for any photographers in range and a visual example of the jarring juxtaposition of Amish transportation with that of modern America.

The buggy is a widely recognized symbol of the Amish, epitomizing Old Order life. It's also a slow-moving road hazard showing up disturbingly often in headlines, usually on the losing end of traffic accidents. Why do the Amish stick to transportation that seems so out of place?

The self-imposed limits on transportation are more than a knee-jerk reaction to modernity or a stubborn toeing the line of tradition. In a sense, Amish bans on ownership of cars and other technologies are rooted in a logical cost-benefit assessment, and spring from values Amish hold dear: family and community.

With ready access to an automobile, Amish worry that driving-age family members would be absent from home more often. Restricting ownership keeps Amish closer to the hearth and more reliant on neighbors, and reduces time spent in urban areas, seen as hotbeds of worldly temptation. The benefit of easy transport is outweighed by the potential threat to family and community. For that matter, Amish do not see automobiles or their drivers as sinful, but they fear what unbridled access to cars could lead to.

Yet Amish readily ride in them—to work, to the store, and to visit distant relatives—which makes some quick to point the finger of hypocrisy. In fact, the charge doesn't really stick: riding as a passenger is certainly less liberating than driving. The relatively high cost of "Amish taxi" service makes Amish think twice before overusing it. And taxis may require planning ahead a few days to reserve a simple ride to the store.

When it comes to the automobile, as with other technologies, Amish have carefully delineated a border between ownership and usage. The buggy not only restricts range but is a cultural symbol. Both as a marker of the people and as a real means of braking the pace of life, horse-drawn transportation continues to fulfill an important function in Amish society.

THE DARK SIDE: WHEN THE CUSTOMER ISN'T RIGHT

A crisp, cloudless February morning, 7:30, and the phone rings. Elam picks up. Not wanting to eavesdrop, I scratch the sleep out of my eyes and focus on the road. I'm behind the wheel of the company vehicle today. Yet I can't help but notice that Elam is doing little talking and a lot of listening. After a minute, the conversation ends, abruptly.

Elam was hung up on by an upset customer, I learn later. Jekyll, whose home, as it happens, we're slated to visit later today, apparently woke up as Hyde. While being chewed out, Elam was informed that all future correspondence should go to the customer's wife.

When the customer, in a more humane incarnation, calls back to apologize, Elam lets out his frustration. And no wonder. The thought of waking up to calls like these can make anyone want to pull up the covers and slam *Snooze*.

Amish businesspeople aim to please. But they also point out the line, a boundary that's crossed when a client starts demanding things outside of a pre-existing agreement or that conflict with an owner's integrity.

Amish are averse to taking legal action, viewing it as a form of aggression. The legal prohibition is taken so seriously that Amish who've instigated suits have found themselves excommunicated. An "evil customer radar" thus comes in handy—whether you're Amish or not—especially if you aim to stay out of court.

Friction can arise, though, when trying to keep people happy. "If the customer wants a piece of siding redone, because he doesn't like the craftsmanship, I'll take it off and redo it," Elam explains. "Now, if the customer insists that I owe him a door, because he decided he wants one, after you gave him the quote . . . I can't just give that to you.

"In a situation like that, is there a winning situation?" he asks.

Lunch stand owner Hannah Stoltzfus, whose clientele is made up 90 percent of the tourist market, cites trying customers as the most challenging part of her business. The most difficult bit, she finds, is having to satisfy demands while keeping a smile on her face.

Another Amishman feels some customers push limits to test you. "You've got to stop them at a certain point," he explains. Some "seem to try you out 'til you don't budge anymore. Then they'll stop. And they like you for it!" he claims. "They want to see what you're going to do."

Pushiness may simply be a hardnosed customer's style of doing business. Regardless, it's wise to determine what is on and off the table before you even get started—both in a contractual and ethical sense.

Business counselor Isaac Smoker explains that "you have to know to what extent you're going to go with your business. You can't be everything to everybody. So at some point, you may have to say no to the customer, or refer them to someone else." Isaac sees scarcity of resources or being asked to compromise a cardinal principle as valid justifications for refusing someone.

Dealing with difficult customers is something that every businessperson must face at some point. This can take compromise and tact. And though it may be difficult to do, it may even involve turning business down.

BOMB SQUAD

Abram Gingerich elaborates on the delicate art of compromise. "There are instances where you just can't help the customer, because he just demands too much from either me, my family, or one of my people." Abram calls this "a balancing act." At the same time, "you have to make him feel that he is right. Even if you can't help him."

Part of the trick is delivering your message—which may mean telling the customer he's wrong—with tact. "There's an art to winning an argument and letting somebody think you lost," another Amish boss points out.

Ivan Miller outlines how he handles less-than-happy people. "You can actually make it a positive," Ivan explains. "You take it on yourself; you tell them you appreciate that they called, and [that] we will promptly take care of that problem." Conceding that you could be at fault often defuses the anger powering the complaint.

And if you're not at fault, it's important to deliver the news in the right way. "If you come back and prove it wasn't you, just tell 'em, 'We could be wrong, but we really checked this out, and . . . we couldn't find anything.'"

Ivan emphasizes humility and understanding, made easier when picturing yourself on the other end of the line. Sometimes just listening and "taking it on yourself"—in a way that you don't immediately admit guilt—is enough to deflate the frustration driving the call.

"It's a matter of getting them to understand—just explaining facts," maintains business vet Nelson Mast. He recalls a dispute where the original issue "was long gone." The argument had become about "who's right . . . who gets to win."

Later, after his employees had backed down and the issue was resolved, the customer chatted with workers and was "just the nicest guy."

"But that didn't come out under pressure," Nelson explains. It's the responsibility of the manager to maintain cool. Nelson trains employees to frame responses in positives. "Never use 'no'," he says. " 'Yes, you have a point, but let me see here . . .' "

Nelson backs his approach with Scripture. "The Bible says, 'Agree with your adversary quickly.' The quicker you find common ground, or find something you agree on, and try and dwell on that, then the other [issue] will start going away."

AVOIDING THEIR ISSUES
AND BAGGAGE

Finding common ground can be trying. "Why is it the ones that really need love the most are often the hardest to love?" one Amishman asks, reflecting on an age-old dilemma.

It's a conundrum Jonas Lapp knows well. Jonas feels that "a key is to not let their issues be your issues."

"Somebody that has issues and is very hard to deal with, they'll do a lot of talking. And if you don't react to that, then you don't play their game."

Some, Jonas admits, can be "very tough to work for. But there again, I think it's because they're trying you out to see how far they can trust you, to see how you react.

"There's red flags that go up," he explains. "I feel you have to draw a boundary line. I can work inside this boundary." Jonas knows what fits inside his line—and what doesn't. "If there's gonna be swearing, dishonesty inside this contract, then I'm out."

If you end up losing the business, then realize you're likely better off for it. Principle trumps extra profit ten times out of ten.

Mervin Riehl refuses to let problem people run him ragged. "There are some customers too that you hardly ever satisfy. Pickier ones. You'll always have them."

One customer demanded that he hand-sort thousands of pieces of product to determine the inevitable fistful of defective ones. Mervin tells such people directly that off-the-wall requests mean a price increase.

"I find that most customers are reasonable [when] you tell 'em up front what you're up against, and where the challenges are gonna be in a job, and what you're thinking you can do to overcome that," Mervin explains. "It just goes a long way.

"There's always some that you'll end up losing. And you know, if you lose them, you just want to make sure that it wasn't because of something you did."

Ultimately, you alone are responsible for managing your attitude in the face of difficult people. "We do have customers that we talk about in the office after we hang up the phone," one Amish entrepreneur admits. "But one thing we've learned already: it doesn't pay to talk negative, because then you act negative, too."

DOING UNTO OTHERS (BEFORE THEY DO UNTO YOU)

The bit about hindsight being crystal clear always sounds smart but never seems too handy after the fact. But is it possible to apply lessons from bad experiences to discern the ones to avoid in the future?

One Amishman describes a "nice young couple" whom he considered friends after a decade-long business relationship. The relationship inexplicably ended with a hefty bad check, and deaf ears when the Amishman tried to collect. For another, the death blow to a long-term association was an unpaid invoice running in the thousands of dollars.

Predicting bad behavior based on typecasting or deciphering signals may be little more than shaky science. But some recall indicators they feel should have tipped them off.

Sometimes, warning signs are obvious from the start. Elam Peachey spends a good bit of time on the phone, following up with clients and taking steps to advance the sales process. His biggest problem? "Handling people that are rude, on the first contact."

Elam's approach is rooted in self-respect. "If they're too rude to answer the phone in a polite fashion, or can't return my phone calls,"

Elam asks, "what's going to happen when we have a problem on the job, or when time comes to pay the invoice?

"Those kind of people, I have actually a hard time dealing with. I tend to just say, 'Alright, you know, forget it.' I don't pursue it."

This cuts down on headaches, Elam says, "*if* you have plenty of work."

Which points up one reality. Screening out customers is not a luxury that all enjoy. But as Elam has learned, saving energy for the positive and polite ones preserves your attitude.

Builder Sam Stoltzfus describes how a contractor brother-in-law fought a long-running battle over a sizable uncollected debt.

Sam feels it's possible to prescreen potential problems. One warning is a person who is extremely detail-oriented, "to the point that it's ridiculous." Sam doesn't neglect details; he simply feels that some can take things "way beyond the level of common sense."

How to handle a prospect fitting that description? "Bid [the job] that high that you don't get it," Sam advises.

When facing demanding people, Nelson Mast tries to "set the limits of what we can do"—by explaining that a given request is outside the company's field of specialization. Nelson then brings the focus back to their strong suits, "so that ... he knows that there's things that we're good at, but he's just happening to be demanding with something."

As far as foretelling problem customers, Nelson feels that "pretending to be a genius in that is a far stretch" though admits that "I've had cases where once we're halfway through ... I should have known not to have [taken] it."

Dennis Miller reflects on the delicacy of the issue. "You have to be careful how you handle those situations. You can't just tell a customer, 'I'm not going to work for you.'"

Similar to Sam Stoltzfus, Dennis suggests flexibility with pricing. He tries to read the signs. If he smells a problem, he might add in his own "grief allowance" to the price of a job. "If I don't get it, let somebody else deal with it."

But when dealing with clients, Dennis feels that at a certain stage, all becomes clear. "You really start knowing what the person is like when you start handing out bills."

DOING UNTO OTHERS

The customer may not always be right, but he's always the customer. Ego-driven bosses find this out pretty quickly when clients begin voting with their feet.

Communication, quality products, reliable service, and maintaining positive perceptions all strengthen the customer bond. Managing these often means managing for the next job. Word of mouth and repeat business spring from the trust and satisfaction created by getting these things right.

Managers and owners must be conscious of their personal and business limits. Learning to deliver "no" or "you're wrong" with tact is an invaluable skill. Refusing problem clients or even cutting them loose may be necessary to preserve sanity, integrity, and financial well-being.

In the next chapter, we begin a two-part look at another crucial relationship managers must tend, particularly as firms develop and grow: that with the employee.

TEN POINTS ON THE CUSTOMER

1. The customer is always right—even when he's wrong. But only up to a point. He stops being right when you have to compromise your integrity or sacrifice your resources beyond a predetermined acceptable level.

2. The Golden Rule goes without saying. Most are tempted to break it at some point.

3. The importance of quality also goes without saying. Protect it, especially when expanding. Expanding too fast can threaten quality and drive away customers.

4. Word of mouth is among the most powerful ways to secure customers. Whether it's furniture, the new dentist, or the latest tech tool, people respond when others they know and trust do the talking. It can be worth losing money to keep a good reputation.

5. Know the 80/20 rule. Focus energies on the top. Spending too much time on the margins can sink an otherwise healthy company.

6. At the same time, don't step on the small. The mighty often start meager, and a trifling request may in fact be a test run for something much more substantial.

7. Customers will tell you what they want, and how to sell it, if you listen. You "listen" in different ways: by scrutinizing sales statistics, by reading news and industry publications, and by old-fashioned asking. You may have to put aside your ego.

8. Unhappy customers talk faster and louder than happy ones. Put out fires quickly. Or better, avoid creating them in the first place by following customer-first principles.

9. Handling difficult customers requires tact and knowledge of how far you'll bend. You may need to avoid or leave destructive customers.

10. At the same time, predictive wizardry is as much art and intuition as it is science. And being choosy is not a luxury available to all.

CHAPTER FIVE

CHOOSING UP SIDES

Getting the Right People in Place

*If you've got a bunch of snobby attitudes . . . forget about it. I don't want to be
part of it. Life is too short.*
—OHIO AMISH ENTREPRENEUR

Tuesday evening. I'm making my way through a corner of hilly
Holmes County. Destination: Ivan Miller's farm. It's frolic time.

At a frolic, Amish combine manpower to complete a work project.
There are quilting frolics and roofing frolics and all sorts of other frolics,
but the best-known frolic is the legendary barn raising, where upwards
of a hundred men erect a barn in a single day. It's a well-coordinated,
precision job, orchestrated by one or two master craftsmen.

Tonight, we're putting siding on a new shop. Ivan and his oldest
son are cooking up another business to add to their present pair of
enterprises. The new venture needs a new building.

Having scooped up a couple of local youth, we arrive at Ivan's to
find the numbers a little low. The group will grow to nearly twenty
by evening's end, as men and boys trickle in after wrapping up duties
at home.

Milling about the barn, I ask repeatedly what my job will be.
I was raised in the city. Put a power tool in my hand and I'm like a
linebacker on a unicycle. Someone's going to get hurt. And since today

I'm masquerading as somebody who might know what he's doing, I'm a bit anxious about sawing off a finger and blowing my cover.

As others arrive, the answer becomes clear: roles fall into place with little discussion. Each does what he's best suited for. In my case that means "pack mule," as one of the men nudges me toward a pile of siding that needs moving. My hosts have a sixth sense for these things, it seems.

I spend most of the evening carrying siding into the shop for the guys with the power tools. Ivan's white-bearded father, a thoughtful, robust seventy-something, partners with me. After proving my mettle as a hauler, I get to swing a hammer a couple of times, feeling like a tough guy but with little to show for it except some holes in the insulation where Ivan really didn't need any.

Ivan, who has recently blown out his back, is relegated to the role of emcee, a job that fits the gregarious Amishman. He spends the evening making the rounds of the shop, offering chocolates and cracking jokes. Chatter and laughter abound, yet the job at hand is taken seriously. The men interweave their separate tasks seemingly without premeditation—each seems to know instinctively what needs doing and who should do it.

The frolic embodies two core elements of Amish society: hard work and community. Work ends well after sundown, topped off with a snack of piping hot coffee (served standard Amish black), corn chips, and rich, gooey raisin bars straight from Ivan's wife's kitchen. As we stand around talking, there's general satisfaction with what was accomplished in three hours. Not the whole job but a necessary piece of it.

Turns out there hasn't been a frolic in this area for awhile. The men have enjoyed it. A grinning Ivan offers thanks all around. The thanks are not really necessary, however. Helping out is just something that you do.

It's worth examining the easy dynamic of the Amish work frolic. They've long ago bought into the idea of teaming for the greater good. They work hard, cooperate, and take ownership in what they do. No one gets paid today. But they know they can expect the same kind of backup should they ever need it.

Amish managers work to build the same dynamic in their businesses. Employees thrive when they feel comfortable and like what they do, and who they do it with. Businesses thrive when employees' objectives are aligned with the owner's.

One part of the formula is getting good people. Another is getting them on board and producing. And a third part is knowing when to cut dead wood.

The Amish managers who follow offer ideas that have worked for them over the long haul. Some have just a handful of workers. The largest employs nearly forty. Their employees are non-Amish as well as Amish.

In this chapter, we'll first look at getting the right people. We'll also examine how to handle the nonproductive ones. Chapter Six will continue the topic, digging deeper into vital management and leadership questions.

TWIDDLING YOUR THUMBS

Glen Beechy, employer of thirty-three, is a modern-day business success story. Seems he's also a full-fledged member of a special club. It's a club that doesn't actually exist, but if it did, we might call it "Thumb-Twiddlers Anonymous."

Glen sits in his office, solid figure comfortable in his executive's chair, a massive desk between us. Workers bang away, toiling on a shop renovation right over our heads. I ask Glen about his day-to-day role in the business.

"Just making sure everything flies," Glen answers, mentioning paperwork, setting hours, and signing checks. "But otherwise, if you ask me what I do in here, I couldn't tell you.

"About a year ago, a fellow comes up to me, a local fellow that has quite a large business. We got to talking; he looked at me and said, 'What do you do, in your business?'

"And I said, 'I'm embarrassed to say.'

" 'No, tell me, what do you do?'

" 'Nothing.'

"And he said, 'You're embarrassed to tell me that?' And I said, 'I am.'

" 'You shouldn't be embarrassed. If you'd have told me you do this, this, and this, I would've told you you're on the wrong track.'

"He said, 'Your job is to do nothing, and just make sure everything *happens*.'

"So I feel a little bit better about it, but still . . . not comfortable with it!" Glen laughs.

Being able to "do absolutely nothing," as Glen puts it, is for many an end goal of business ownership.

Thumb-twiddling is nothing to be ashamed of. Thumb-twiddling isn't *really* about sitting around doing nothing. It's greasing the wheels, pinch-hitting, and keeping the cobwebs out of the corners, to use a few of the folksy management phrases that get batted around the community.

As Glen's example shows, business success takes figuring out a formula that works and then getting the right people in place to execute it. But it's not automatic. It takes getting comfortable with delegation.

ONE TEST ALONE

"I delegate things out. We have extremely good help. A lot of times, they will know more than I do. I believe in trusting people. And it works." Ivan Miller points out that delegation can be challenging if your head's not right for it. He explains how tough it was for him early on.

"People used to ask for [product manager] Sarah Schrock. I was like, 'Guys, I'm the boss here, okay?!' I didn't tell 'em, but that's how I felt. It didn't take me long to figure out, this is really what I want!" Ivan chuckles. "A person that can actually handle things better than I can. But in the beginning it was something to work through.

"A lot of the problems small business owners have—they'll hire somebody in, but they think they have to make all the decisions. . . . I thought I had to be the one who looked good.

"But for a business owner to look good, he doesn't have to make all the decisions. He's just got to stay in business for ten years."

Sounds simple enough.

Simple, but not easy.

As Ivan makes clear, the bottom line tells all.

If the business goes down in flames, no one remembers all the nice messages over the intercom. It doesn't matter that you scraped ice off the wings, served drinks, and checked the landing gear while it plummeted. The business is dead. No one cares.

Delegation is what you should have been doing instead. The hard part is letting go of a piece of something you've invested so much in.

Ohio furniture finisher Harley Stutzman explains, "It's a hard thing—and I trust my employees—but it's a hard thing to let go. I used to do it all. Now I'm supposed to step back and say, okay, I'll let these guys do it, and I have to have enough faith that they're going to put out the quality of product that I want."

The vicious odor of wood varnish pops my nostrils as it wafts into the office where Harley and I sit. I wonder what it's like to toil away the day immersed in the headache-inducing fumes. Harley's nine workers—from a pair of teenage girls to his sixty-something father—wear facemasks. A filtration system shuttles noxious air out of the shop.

Harley's lazy eyes and subdued tone mask an intensity that had him working double-time and skimping on groceries to get his business to lift off. Harley started his finishing shop nearly a decade ago with the dream of being able to work at home with his children and wife around.

All things considered, it's worked out pretty well. Harley has seen growth every year since starting, even when others have had down years.

But delegation has been a hang-up—really, *the* hang-up. Harley calls it "one of my biggest obstacles in growth."

Others, like Glen Beechy, agree.

"That's one of the biggest challenges in running a business ... matching the right people to the right job skills," Glen explains from his commander's seat. There are different ways to get hold of the good ones. Glen likes to home-develop talented individuals. He's enjoyed the good fortune of having reliable people with him from the beginning.

At the same time, Glen is not afraid to go after key people in other companies. A lot of his foremen "are the people we picked and chose because we felt they could do a better job and advance, better than some of the other people."

Glen says it's not too hard to figure out who fits in and who doesn't.

"Unfortunately, not everybody takes ownership.... You basically try and pick out the good ones and hang on to those.... The rest of them, if they don't buy into the concept of the way you run your business ... they'll go away."

Delegation is inevitable as a business grows. And who you hire to fill key roles matters. Which brings up a few questions. How to go about picking out "the good ones"? And just who do the Amish consider the good ones to be?

But first, a look at the growth question itself—namely, when to do it. Assuming that increasing your business's size aligns with your business vision, what conditions must exist to make growth a wise decision? Amish have varying opinions. One answer involves not only dollars and cents but management capacity as well.

WHICH WAY TO THE PEACHEY PLACE?

There are over eight hundred Miller households in the northern Indiana settlement. One quarter of all Amish families in Lancaster County answer to Stoltzfus. In Holmes County, Ohio, you'll find forty-seven David Yoders.

It's enough to make even the Amish scratch their heads at times.

With relatively closed communities, a small number of surnames, and a tendency to pick from a limited pool of first names, more than a few Amish end up with identical mailbox tags.

So if you're trying to track someone down in Amish America, it helps to know more than just a first and last name.

If you are one of the thousands of Amish in the Daviess County settlement in southern Indiana, there's nearly a 9 in 10 chance your last name is one of just six. Daviess County has perhaps the highest naming homogeneity of any major Amish community.

Nicknames help. In Daviess, you might belong to the Nip, Choke, or Bottle bloodlines or any of the other family-line monikers. Your occupation might help to track you down as well—most days, everybody knows where to find "Printer Al."

Amish parents run through a laundry list of standard first names for their new additions. Some of them can be tongue-twistingly similar: Ervin, Mervin, Marvin, Marlin, Merlin, and Verlin show up frequently in some Midwestern settlements. When they are all Millers—the most common Amish surname—it only adds to the confusion.

Initials help as well. One Amishman was compelled by his workplace to adopt an extra middle letter because two other workers had the same name. In any case, the initial comes in handy off the job too: five others like him live in his settlement.

Familial pairings help out too: you might be Eli's John, or "Bill" Barb Hochstetler in the example of an Ohio midwife whose bishop husband's name set her apart from all the other Barb Hochstetlers.

And spelling often varies: Beechy is also seen as Beachy or Beachey; Fry can be spelled Frey or Frye; and Hershberger exists as Herschberger and Harshberger.

To help sort things out, the Amish produce detailed directories which provide maps, addresses, and birthdates. The directory lets you know when to send a card or how to get to church service.

Amish directories are usually updated every five to seven years. The one for Holmes County, Ohio, has over eight hundred pages. The Amish joke that the directory is out of date before it's even printed, since they're always moving, marrying, or having children.

MANAGEMENT AND THE EXPANSION CHALLENGE

How to know when to grow? Many answers revolve around a key theme: expansion should depend on your personal business vision. Which means that for some, getting bigger is a bad idea. For others, it's a main plank of the vision.

Pennsylvania builder Elam Peachey sees expansion as a function of both management capacity and income potential. In his equation, extra employees do not automatically equal extra income.

"I have four employees and myself. And I make *x* amount of dollars. . . . [An] acquaintance of mine had twelve employees and made half of what I was [making].

"To me, bigger is not better there. . . . I'm not necessarily on a power trip. I don't need to have fifteen people under my thumb.

"So as far as I'm concerned," Elam continues, "it's the income that controls 'bigger is better.'. . . If I can make more money with six people, that's great. I could hire someone tomorrow and increase my income, I think, *if it was the right person*.

"If all I do is . . . spend six months training him, and six months picking up the pieces after him, and six months maybe making a few dollars on him, then he quits, it didn't help me any."

Elam says it's also important to know whether "you have the effective leadership" before hiring someone new.

"If you hire a guy, are you going to be able to effectively manage them all? If the answer is definitely yes, and having an extra guy is going to result in extra income—go ahead.

"Now, if the answer is . . . no, I can't manage them all—but these two guys can take care of this department. . . . [Well,] can they?

"Before I hire six new people, I've got to have people to help train them and manage them. . . . You can't hire somebody today, even if he was a leader in another organization—you can't expect him to lead your organization tomorrow. You need a little bit of a grace period to ease into it."

As far as placing people in the right roles and developing managers and leaders, Elam says that "you need to meet their skill levels, so you can pay their skill levels—and keep them satisfied. But on the other hand, if you push 'em too hard—they're out of their comfort zone each and every day—they're not happy either." Elam prefers to err on the side of pushing people forward later than sooner.

Oddly, the non-driving, pacifist Amish seem to favor armed forces and automobile metaphors, at least when explaining things to the English world. "It's kind of like the military," summarizes Elam, accordingly. "If you don't have the lieutenants and the sergeants and so forth . . . you can't have privates."

FITTING THE TEMPLATE

When recruiting their privates and sergeants and lieutenants, Amish business owners usually have a specific picture in mind and gauge each potential hire against that template.

Ohio contractor Dan Troyer is of the same mind as others when it comes to delegation: he cites "having competent people around you" as the most important element to his success. Dan's people "have a lot of responsibility." And in making his picks, he looks carefully at a few factors.

"You need a certain amount of talent. You have to have a good attitude," Dan explains. "Experience is a plus," but "you have to have a mix of it. You can't have a guy with a lot of talent and a good attitude just jumping in at any job. But those are the people you want to grow in the company. That's the best way to do it if possible."

For those used to the job-seeker's minefield of psychological testing, second- and third- and fourth-round interviews, and requests for references going back to kindergarten, the approach of some Amish to hiring might seem quaint.

Visual clues, gut feelings, and first impressions factor heavily in the equation. These methods may seem haphazard and nonobjective. "You hire for character and train for the job," says a three-decade veteran with two dozen on payroll. Sometimes—often—the gut is the most reliable tool to gauge that character.

READING THE SIGNS

Pennsylvania Amish builder Jonas Lapp clearly loves life. And people. One of nine brothers, he's well on his way to building his own thriving clan.

Jonas and I sit at his kitchen table as the children tear up the house around us, in anticipation of a game of Monopoly set to commence the moment I walk out the door. Outsiders praise wide-eyed Amish youngsters for their good behavior. But kids will be kids, and Jonas's are a bit rowdy tonight.

Jonas has had his share of struggles in business. Yet his relationships have brought him much joy. Along the way he's developed an eye for people.

"I think the way a person walks says a lot about what's happening in his life. That's kind of the first thing you see," says Jonas. "If the person kinda slouches and is just kind of shuffling, there's probably not a whole lot of self-esteem there."

The other thing it tells you, according to Jonas, is " 'Now I don't really need this job'—there's really no vision there," Jonas explains. "So you're trying to read the signs."

Jonas finds that having the opportunity to work with people and help them through their own hang-ups is one of the greatest rewards of being in business. And that requires holding them to a higher standard while challenging them to grow. "This is a team," says Jonas. "Are you gonna come ready to play? Or do you want to sit on the bench?" Jonas asks.

While that may sound harsh, Jonas also realizes that many people he comes across have untapped potential. They often just need someone to push them. So while paying close attention to the signs, he tries not to rule anyone out right off. "You give people a chance, you know?"

Ohio stonemason Jason Glick takes an approach similar to Jonas's. "Gut feeling and more the way the person actually is, is a big thing to me.

"If I see that he's willing to learn, or change, if it's not exactly what I think that he should be for us, I would hire him—if I see that he's willing to change."

Jason also cites the importance of "a clean atmosphere." He measures new people against how well he feels they'd fit into the environment he tries to maintain. "That's one thing I always drill new guys [about] before I hire them.

"We work for these people in these big expensive allotments," Jason explains. "I always look at it from my standpoint—if I'd have a house and I'd come out and see somebody standing on the porch, and [an] empty can of beer, and smoking and cussing—I mean, get out of here.

"So we *really* try to enforce a clean environment ... and always treat that employer—the homeowner—with utmost respect. You have to. I mean, they're putting bread on your table."

EXPERIENCE VERSUS THE "BLANK PAGE"

Is a thick résumé always all it's cracked up to be? As we saw in Chapter Two, many Amish think not.

"We don't care how much experience he has," says Pennsylvania Amishman Mose Fisher. "We'll train him. I'd sooner train a guy than [if he had] ten years of experience—because then we can train him the way we want him."

Mose partners with two brothers to run a successful contracting company. Mose and his brothers want to enjoy the company of the people they'll potentially be spending a large chunk of their time with. More than experience, Mose values attitude. He can tell who appeals to him fairly quickly.

"I can soon tell if he comes in what for attitude he has. I'll bring him in—[find out] what they do, what they like—I'll just talk to him for an hour or so. And when he goes out the door ... I know a little bit [about him]."

Mose's wife helps out. He takes the opinion of his significant other into account, as do many of his peers. "There was something she didn't like about the guy," Mose says about one hire. "He didn't turn out so good either," he admits.

As with other Amish, Mose has a certain paradigm he tries to match. Knowing beforehand what's important to him in an employee, he can usually tell fairly quickly if a given candidate fits the bill.

Mose speaks fondly of a non-Amish university student who became a driver in his company. The student attended the local Bible college and wished to fill some free time.

"Well, that right there told me, this guy's going to college; he's paying his college ... he's doing what he has to do," says Mose. "It never spited me that we hired that guy."

Mose also looks for people who are fun. Another student he hired brought a lot of joy to the company through his sense of humor.

"He's really a ... character. When he came, he didn't know a thing about construction." That didn't matter. "I don't care; I don't even want to see their college degree.... I don't care what you learned in school ... your attitude [is what counts]."

PICKING UP THE BROOM

I've finally caught gazebo maker Reuben Detweiler, who spends a good chunk of time out on jobs, at home. Reuben resides in an extremely entrepreneurial corner of his community, with five Amish-run businesses on his mile alone.

A jovial father of five, Reuben admits to enjoying talk radio whenever he gets a chance—which usually means only when riding with an English person.

Reuben is quite a talker himself. Our conversation takes in everything from presidential politics (Republican) to premarital sex (against) to quitting smoking (tough). Reuben also spends time reviewing important characteristics of an employee.

Most Amish want workers who exemplify a few fundamental character traits. The sense of duty to work, for example, is one that makes Amish highly valued employees. Recognizing this, manufacturers have concentrated production near Amish areas to tap into the ethic. If you own any sort of recreational vehicle, for example, there's a decent chance that Amish hands helped assemble it: the "RV capital of the world" is located in a major Amish settlement in Indiana.

Reuben exemplifies the Amish mentality regarding work. As he tells it, it's that something inside that gets you out of bed every day: "I love working. I got two hands, I'm healthy, and I love getting up in the morning knowing I got a job to go to. That is a blessing in itself—just being able to work.

"If somebody doesn't like to work, and always thinks of it as drudgery, and makes himself believe he doesn't like it, he's not going to enjoy himself. He's going to have a miserable life," the Amishman decrees.

In Amish America, work translates into dignity and self-worth. Sitting in Reuben's office, I offer a theoretical scenario that another business owner had earlier shared: *College kid, highly educated, comes around the shop looking for a job. Owner hands him a broom and tells him to start sweeping. College kid refuses, seeing such work as being beneath him.*

Reuben is quick to respond: "If he's not dignified enough to pick up that broom, he wouldn't be dignified enough to work for me. He has ... pretty low self-esteem."

Paraphrasing a biblical passage, Reuben states that "the humble people will be honored, and the people that want the honor will be chastised."

"He's probably a very highly educated man. But it's really sad to say that by not picking up that broom, he saw himself as way better than the guy who has the job [for him].

"If we're not on the same level, it's not gonna work. If he despises that broom that much, from the get-go, well he just proved ... his expectations are way beyond what that guy had. He's got to go somewhere else to find what he's looking for."

ROUND PEG, SQUARE HOLE

Outsiders praise the perceived idyllic serenity of "Amish Country"—the rural harmony, agrarian bliss, the blessed peace and quiet. But if you've been anywhere near an Amish furniture shop, with its diesel engines and noisy machinery, you know that "blessed peace and quiet" ain't quite what it used to be. At the same time, harmony and cohesion remain prime virtues in Amish society and, by extension, Amish business.

Reuben, like many, is not afraid to cut employees who disrupt the workplace dynamic.

Reuben describes such a problem with a worker who did a good job but "got the impression that I treat everybody different than him. And the *reason* for that is because *he's* the guy we had to treat different.

"We had to treat him with gloved hands. We had to watch what we say; we had to watch what we do; we had to watch that we don't make him mad.

"He created a lot of dissension in my company. I fired him. I let him go. I wasn't mean; I said, 'I can't do it. It won't work.' I felt sorry for him. There's no doubt he could have been a good worker, but again, he didn't want to pick up the broom.

"He wanted to start above where I'm at, and that won't work with me. Not because I'm the boss," Reuben says, but because "you can be taught it, you can see it, you can know how it feels, but you can never learn it until you actually do it."

Reuben's impression of higher learning is similar to that of many Amish. While not exactly contemptuous of university training, most tend to find it a bit overrated. Amish recognize that their quality of life would be diminished without the services of educated outsiders. It's just that the cocky college type, by his very nature, tends to prick at Amish sensibilities.

Reuben likes to punctuate his points with stories and anecdotes. "Years ago, President Roosevelt, he had a ranch out West," he begins. "And one day he was out helping his foreman and the cowboys round up calves. And he came to a place where there was a calf in the herd, and it was obvious it was the neighbor's calf. And the foreman told him . . . we could just brand that and the neighbor'd never know it. Then it's ours.

"You know what? He fired that man. He said if a man steals *for* you, he will steal *from* you. And that is true."

Honesty, work ethic, compatibility—all are highly valued by Amish. When hiring, skills and experience, which are easier to acquire than a good conscience, tend to take a back seat, especially when one of the above three qualities is missing. Character comes out a clear winner.

An Ohio sawmill owner sums it up well: "I would rather have a good worker, that gets along with people, than an excellent worker, who doesn't get along with people. If you want to ask what I look for, I look for a person who wants to be a part of it."

DOUBLY BLESSED

So where do all the people come from? One factor is the sky-high Amish birth rate, which clocks in at about seven children per family, versus a general population norm of just over two.

A good number of those births bring twice the blessing. Along with the yam-eating Yoruba people of Western Nigeria, the Amish rank near the top among ethnic subgroups when it comes to twinning, exhibiting one of the highest rates in the world.

Brad Igou, editor of *The Amish in Their Own Words*, points to a Berne *Tri-weekly News* article reporting that the Adams/Allen County and Lagrange County, Indiana, settlements register a whopping 21.1 sets of twins per 1,000 births, about 30 percent higher than the general population. A few families in these communities have two or three sets of twins—even four sets have occurred.

Hereditary tendencies get amplified among the closed-community Amish. This also means that certain extremely rare diseases show up more frequently.

Because of this, special clinics have been set up to diagnose and treat rare ailments. Dr. Holmes Morton runs a Lancaster County clinic that treats Amish and Mennonite children suffering from sixty different genetic conditions.

Marriage norms exist. First-cousin marriages are taboo, though Amish spouses may be related more distantly. Amish living in smaller communities may be forced to search outside of their home settlement for a mate.

The Amish are still highly interrelated. Almost all the thirty thousand Amish in Lancaster County descend from just a few dozen eighteenth-century immigrant families. It's not unusual to find marriage partners who are second or third cousins. Or as an Amish father once joked, "We've got the family trees that don't fork."

In any case, children of Amish unions are anything but a burden in a society that takes the "Go forth and multiply" decree to heart. Besides providing useful helping hands with the many house, shop, or farming tasks, children are seen as blessings from God.

Or as one Amish mother put it—repeating a sentiment common among her peers—"our children are the only treasures we can take with us to heaven."

TRICKLE-DOWN ATTITUDE

How about a few "attitude platitudes"? *Attitude is everything. Attitude determines altitude. Attitude is infectious.* And so on. From greeting cards to head coaches, we're bombarded by the message that attitude matters.

But for a reason. And in business, especially, the keen manager is careful to remember the trickle-down effect of attitude. The people you employ are the public face of your firm. Employees often have more direct contact with the customer than the boss does. Good bosses know to set the tone for new hires from the very start.

"When I hire a new girl in, I have about a ten, fifteen minute . . . prep session," says Ivan Miller, "and I tell 'em, . . . in the morning, when we get here, . . . we ask everybody how are you this morning, and they better have a good [attitude]."

Ivan's business handles calls from his many customers—retail shops scattered around the country. Ivan realizes how important the voice on the other end of the line is for a customer. Especially when he'll probably never get to meet that customer in person.

"The thing is, people on the phone . . . wanna know, how are you? They're not asking if you got a bellyache, headache, or snotty nose; they want to know, how's your attitude? How's life?

"Attitude's a choice," Ivan continues. "And I tell 'em, you won't get fired as quickly for your performance as you do for your attitude. . . . We want smiles, and we want good attitudes. If you can handle that, we want you. If you can't—out the door."

Ivan sets expectations. And more importantly, he sets a personal example. Pitching in at Ivan's frolic, I witnessed it firsthand. The captain affects the crew. No one worth their salt sticks around too long if they know they can get better treatment somewhere else.

Ivan, like Mose Fisher, is in business not just to get the bills paid but to enjoy it as well. He knows that the people he surrounds himself with will affect not only the bottom line but how much he loves life.

"You don't have to be with a guy long [to figure it out]," says homebuilder Ezra Miller. "If you're with a guy for a month, and all he does is 'f—this' all the time, . . . you're gonna be doing it yourself. Without thinking. It's gonna come whether you want it to or not."

Ezra says that "it doesn't take long" to figure out someone's story. "It's funny, I had a man come in here. . . . I was looking for a guy, and I had about four or five of 'em come in, and the one . . . he comes in here and says, 'Well, I need twenty dollars an hour to start.'

"And I had [another] come in here . . . and he says, 'Hey, I just need a job; I want to work. After a week or two, you pay me what I'm worth.'

"You see the difference? And it doesn't take long [to know]."

YOU'RE NOT MARRIED TO ME

Do there exist dark souls who actually enjoy distributing pink slips? Letting someone go is near the bottom of most managers' lists of tasks. Firing employees can perhaps be largely avoided. "Hopefully, by hiring right in the first place, and then treating them right, you just never have to go there," says one veteran.

But even with exceptional hiring and stellar management, you still may find yourself having to go there. Amish graybeard Menno Graber, bishop, father, and long-haul furniture man, has spent a large part of his life working with, and through, others. "There's a difference in employees. Some are worth more than the others!" Menno says. "When we hire, we tell them, [you're] going to get paid just like you work. And if you wanna goof off, you won't get a raise. And we were paying our girls real good money, because we had some real good ones." Like many Amish furniture shop owners, Menno employs women for certain jobs, such as furniture finishing work or secretarial tasks.

"And, you know, we had a couple that ... I sometimes thought maybe we'd just be better off [for them] to stay home and pay 'em!

"Once in a while you get one that ... can't chew gun and work at the same time," the Amishman continues. "I always think that if I start them low enough, and if they don't produce, and you don't give them a raise, they'll leave." Menno's tone drops. He obviously takes little pleasure in talking about this part of the job. "So that way you don't have to tell them, 'Well, I can't use you.'

"If you don't get a raise, you kind of think to yourself, 'Well, I'm not doing the job.' "

Menno's nonconfrontational approach may not be best for everyone, but it seems to work for him. Being a bishop, Menno likely has it tougher than others. Probably more than anyone else, an Amish person in his delicate position is forced to balance obligations to the business with those to the community.

The famed tightness of the Amish community can make personnel decisions more complicated. It's one thing issuing walking papers to the random hire who's been on since last Thursday. But when it's your neighbor, or cousin, or brother, it can be a totally different story.

"It's a little tougher in our community—we live in the same neighborhoods they do; we go to the same church these guys do," explains Glen Beechy. "Everything we do is centered around family and friends and stuff—church people and neighbors. If I don't like one of my employees, I just can't go up and fire him because I don't like him, or he didn't do his job, because that can come back to haunt me."

Glen differs from Menno in his approach, preferring to hit things head-on. "If somebody is doing things that they shouldn't be doing, or we need to change things, I point-blank talk to them. And I tell them right up front, 'You're not married to me; if you don't like what I'm trying to do here, that's okay.'

" 'I want to make you happy, but if I can't, that's okay.' I don't try to hang on to them just to hang on to them so that they don't leave. I let them go if they don't like it."

There's a reason being straightforward is so essential. "I'm right up front with everybody," Glen explains, "because I have family here. I have brothers-in-law, and I have brothers here. . . . I keep it on a very professional level—at *work*."

America is filled with family businesses. When you work with family, adjustable boundaries keep things functional, at work and at home.

Glen continues, "When we get away from work, I am not their boss. . . . I totally turn it on and off. You have to. See, as an employee I hold them out here," he gestures, "and when I get away from the workplace, I remove that."

"There are some that try to take advantage of you then," Glen chuckles, "trying to get the inside track!"

DUKING IT OUT

Amish try to weed out people that cause conflict or bring unsavory elements into a business. But situations arise where the judgment call isn't so cut-and-dried.

Is it the boss's job to moderate interpersonal conflicts at work, to micromanage each relationship? Some Amish have an eye for placing workers who mesh well together. Some try to rotate them in order to promote the spread of ideas around the organization. Ezra Miller explains how he manages his eighteen men.

"I shake mine up a good bit. . . . I think you can probably get *too* used to each other."

Ezra says his foremen do things in different manners and that "they need to be able to adjust. . . . It gets them to give up and not always think, this is the one way to do it."

Joe Yoder, an Ohio furniture maker with over three dozen workers, emphasizes the importance of first getting employees' okay before moving them around—or at least raising the idea with the person rather than suddenly shifting him from one job to the next. That way, workers feel that their opinion matters as well.

Talking about a recent switch, Joe explains that one worker "kind of made his own choice on that. And that's what I want." On the lookout for greater efficiencies, Joe moves employees for productivity and to fill holes, as well as for workplace cohesion.

Since conflict often stems from personality clashes, sometimes a simple personnel reshuffle gets the job done. Mose Fisher has occasionally had more drastic situations to deal with. Workers butt heads. Mose has twenty-two of them. His approach? "Change 'em."

"We had a driver that couldn't get along with anybody. So he's my driver." An older fellow, "he just can't take the orders off of the younger guys," Mose explains, so he removed him from that environment. Though Mose didn't have to, something in this person compelled him to give him another chance, even though he's walked off multiple jobs.

But when lines have been definitively crossed, Mose relies on a tool that makes firing situations clear-cut and objective. That tool is the employee handbook.

The handbook, which Mose drew up with the assistance of a legal advisor, outlines rules and expectations. It details which offenses get written warnings, and which are immediately "fire-able." Employees read and sign it before being brought on. One benefit of the handbook is that it gives employees a clear idea of expectations. Another is in preventing unwarranted unemployment claims.

But conflict does not necessarily have to lead to someone getting fired. When tempers flare, other bosses get creative with their employees. One furniture shop owner has a simple formula for resolving issues.

"We have very little conflicts, but when there are conflicts, I put it back in their hands. I say, 'What do you think?' A lot of times they answer their own problem."

RESPECT ON THE LINE

Jason Glick, stonemason, has come a long way as a manager over his nine years in the business. Part of that development has been in learning how to let people go.

How many has he fired?

"A *lot* of them already," Jason chuckles. "We went through 'em."

Jason cites lack of respect as the biggest reason people get the axe—lack of respect for coworkers, employer, and equipment, all of which is supplied by Jason at his own cost.

Jason says you usually recognize the bad ones pretty quickly. "I give them one warning, and I tell them it's coming if things don't change."

At the same time, Jason says, "I try not to be too harsh. I try to . . . let them know what needs to be corrected." But once he makes the decision, Jason stands firm. "Once I say you're outta here if things don't change, then that's the way it's gonna be. You know, don't try to get away with it.

"And I've really developed that just in the years of being in business, because my first couple years . . . I just couldn't . . . lay down the law and fire somebody. Actually, the first couple guys I fired . . . I just laid them off, and didn't hire them back," Jason admits. "I just didn't have what it took."

For Jason, it was a process of "developing into more of a businessperson and realizing how serious this was."

He now sees the benefits of being firm. "It seems it's much better," he explains. "I mean, my relationship with my employees is better than it ever was. Just because I think they have a lot more respect for me. Just because you're more serious."

Jason knows that the minute you compromise and go back on your word, people start to walk all over you.

"People know if you're a pushover, if they can get away with things. . . . It's pretty much like kids with their mom and dad," Jason grins.

CHOOSING UP SIDES

When it comes to hiring and firing, the Amish emphasize direct dealings and straight shooting.

Qualifications factor into the equation but aren't everything. Gut feelings matter.

Amish tend to deal with employee problems efficiently and quickly. A family atmosphere prevails in the typical workshop—a definite strength, though it introduces issues the Amish must deal with delicately.

Harmony and cohesiveness are highly valued. Amish know you can change a person's skill level a lot more easily than you can change her character. At the same time, they realize that no one is perfect. Amish business owners hold the door open for people who have their hearts in the right place.

Let's assume you've got the right people. In the next chapter, we'll examine how to keep them around, keep them happy, and keep them performing.

TEN POINTS ON HIRING AND FIRING

1. At a certain point, trying to do it all yourself is a recipe for disaster. There is one test of success in business—not whether you made all the decisions, but did the company prosper?

2. You create your environment, and your environment creates you. Pick your people with that in mind.

3. When hiring, be clear with yourself on what character traits are most important. How will new people fit in with current employees? With elements of your vision?

4. Know what you need in skills and experience, but don't be afraid to trust intuition.

5. Select the less-skilled person with a desire to do well and who will promote harmony over the ultra-skilled one with a poor attitude. Ability can be acquired, but a sour work environment is tough to fix.

6. Education does not equal character. Your best workers may not necessarily have fancy qualifications. Don't automatically rule out the good person with less-impressive credentials.

7. Your example counts. Like attracts like. If your attitude stinks, don't be surprised if your employees' do too.

8. Conflict can sometimes work itself out on its own. But you may have to step in, be creative, and mix things up.

9. Keep bad apples out. Fire people who poison the work environment.

10. Be fair when giving warnings and second chances. But if you decide to fire someone, don't back down. Your integrity and your employees' respect are on the line.

CHAPTER SIX

FISHING LESSONS

Empowering Your Most Valuable Asset

You can control a company in two ways: fear—or with respect.
—LANCASTER AMISH BUILDER

E zra Miller runs a construction firm with up to four projects going on at any given time. The upbeat Lancaster Amishman is no stranger to challenges in the business. One thing Ezra doesn't have a problem with, though, is employee turnover.

With eighteen on payroll, he estimates the average worker has been with the company nine years. "Everybody talks about my men. All the time," Ezra declares. "Yelling at each other out at the job, laughing, having a good time. And not with any swearing, cussing and being upset at each other. Just good clean fun."

Ezra knows his employees are extremely important to his success. Making employees feel a part of a greater whole, getting them to see a higher purpose, and rewarding them accordingly are all vital to keeping them with the company.

The "employees are your most important asset" idea may be more valid today than ever. "Every company has access to the same physical resources," writes Paul Brown for the *New York Times*. "Today, technology is basically a commodity, and thanks to the Internet and overnight shipping, location is substantially less important than it was. That leaves workers as the only true source of competitive advantage."

Many of the most successful Amish entrepreneurs would agree, and it's here that they often have a real competitive advantage. This is partially due to whom Amish hire, but picking the right people is only part of the playbook. Once they get them on board, they know how to keep them around and get them to produce to their potential.

This second part of our look at people examines how to get the most out of your employees. And just as importantly, how to do it so they love you for it and want to stay.

We start with the importance of communication in the business context, and the "employee as extended family" ideal typical among Amish. We'll next examine philosophies common to Amish culture on how to best motivate employees.

Finally, we'll size up various financial and nonfinancial means of compensation. Taken together, these elements—communication, motivation, compensation—help keep employees happy, productive, and staying a valuable part of your thriving organization.

CHEMISTRY CLASS

Orie Hershberger is talking chemistry. "Same as a ball team," he begins in his mellow drawl. "Look at the New York Yankees. They go out and buy [their players]. Money. It doesn't really do it.

"Chemistry does it," says Orie. "You take a team that plays together. Each one is there to pick the other guy up. It's just a whole lot better; there's a better working atmosphere there. It just all falls into place.

"Same way as you would have a family," the fifty-something Santa-faced sawmill owner continues, as his wife sharpens saw blades in a corner of the shop. "You want to create something where the people *want* to come to work, instead of *have to* come to work."

Tomorrow is pizza day. It's an extra expense, but "they look forward to it, it's better than always packing a lunch." Orie feels it creates a "relaxed atmosphere."

Orie acknowledges plentiful ways to make people feel appreciated—"just jumping in there, helping myself . . . there are all kinds of things that you can create, [to] show them that you really do care for them." Ultimately, Orie feels, it comes down to perception: how a manager views his people.

"I've heard this term so much in the business world—'all you need is a warm body.' That's a very common term," he concedes. "I just don't want to *ever* get in a situation where I think that a person is just a warm body."

AN EXTENSION OF FAMILY

The warm-body syndrome strikes when the manager sees employees as little different from widgets or chocolate chips or any other input on the list. Employees and their output can, of course, be tallied in endless ways.

Numbers are important. An effective manager must grasp his organization's quantifiables. But when managing people, numbers are but a piece of the patchwork.

Amish business thinking reflects community. Employees are fellow church members, in-laws, cousins, neighbors. In Amish America, the familial aspect comes preinstalled. Yet that doesn't mean it can't be programmed into the non-Amish firm.

THE SILO RING

The hand-scrawled note on the door said he'd be at the neighbor's, "to the South."

It's early autumn and harvest time in northern Indiana. I've got a load of books to deliver, and I'm looking for Leon.

As I pull my loaded-down pick-up into the neighbor's barnyard, I spot an older Amishman angled over a cane. Easing off the gas, I roll down the window and inquire as to Leon's whereabouts.

After starting to explain, the wiry old-timer suggests he just show me himself. He seems keen on getting a lift, and I'm glad to offer it. Grandpa hops into the shotgun seat and points the way over the bumpy fields.

As we turn the corner, the crew comes into view—a mighty team of eight Belgian draft horses, each weighing in at nearly a ton, hauling a bulky silage-cutter. Four or five Amishmen hustle like mad to stack the rapidly falling corn sheaves onto the wagon as the brawny beasts power forward.

The men have been at it a couple hours already this forenoon. Once they've flattened these fields, they'll be off to the next, as over the coming weeks the corn melts away across the community, leaving stripped-bare fields in place of oceans of iridescent gold-green stalks.

"Silo rings" consist of a few, usually neighboring farmers who pitch together to get the dirty, backbreaking job done. At silo time, Amish put in solid eight- to ten-hour days, and still get home in time for milking. The toughest job is catching and stacking the sheaves as they shoot in off the chopper, while maintaining a precarious balance as the wagon trundles the uneven field. Meanwhile, the pile grows, leaving increasingly meager space to maneuver. Silo-filling time is also a time of accidents.

But with corn down and crop stores brimming, you sense a feeling of accomplishment—and dare to say, a touch of near-pride—listening to Amish farmers recount the tonnage packed away that day.

Over a period of weeks, the silo ring rotates from one farm to the next, making huge, unwieldy jobs more manageable. For Amish, it's not only a practical solution to an agricultural challenge; it's a chance at camaraderie and symbolic of a connected brotherhood of tenders of the land. Farmers depend on one another to achieve the results they need at the crucial time of harvest.

Similarly, in Amish businesses employees are often regarded as extended family. Owners depend on workers and vice versa. And Amish bosses do their part to create close ties.

Family, of course, starts at home. The Amish remember that their employee is usually also a spouse to someone, and often a parent to a hefty handful—before being a worker. Ohio furniture man Alvin Hershberger explains.

"I know one thing: I want my employees to go home feeling good that they did something that day.

"If they go home not feeling good, if it's a man, and he's got a wife and children at home, what kind of experience are they going to have when he comes home?" Alvin asks.

What do your employees really care about? Odds are that family is at or near the top of the list. Wise bosses incorporate this natural human concern into their approach.

Managers have more to do than fret the day away over employees' moods. Yet Alvin feels the good boss can still take an active role, which may come in a few simple words: "Hey, today didn't go too good. . . . We screwed up here, we screwed up there—forget about it!"

Some believe in actively engaging employees' families. This may mean simply keeping in touch with loved ones, particularly spouses. Employees need to know that "what's going on in their family is very important to you. Because when it's not going good in their family, then it's not gonna be good at work," says Jonas Lapp.

"If they're married . . . or he has a fiancée or a girlfriend, if that fellow's important in your business, let their helpmate know, that your husband is doing a wonderful job, and he's very important in my business."

Practically speaking, Jonas suggests that you "make a point, if a guy does something exceptional, maybe works a Saturday when they were gonna have a vacation . . . and he sacrificed, personally go out and thank that lady," Jonas says, "and maybe a gift card."

Such gestures "absolutely" make an impact. "It's very tough if a woman has to suffer and doesn't get acknowledged."

KEEPING THEM BUSY

The typical Amish business owner is reluctant to lay people off. Employers hustle to get work in slow times, often mainly so that workers can remain busy and continue bringing in a paycheck.

One entrepreneur describes weathering a slow spell. "We made benches; we made anything we could ... [to] put in auctions, just to keep my workers 'til things picked up. It didn't really make money, but it was enough to pay for my employees."

A shop owner shows similar consideration for his ten workers. "If you hire people and they're making payments on a home, you don't want to lay them off. . . . They have bills to pay."

An Amishman who's recently added help echoes the concern: "It's a whole different story ... you've got all of a sudden nine families to feed, instead of two."

Their thinking may seem quaint. When a company caves in or the economy falters, the ensuing layoffs are hardly shocking. Shedding workers is a universally accepted way to survive difficult periods. Amish are not immune to business realities. Yet the community dynamic encourages treating employees as more than just another input.

Firing someone you've known since childhood is a lot harder than canning the anonymous face. Perhaps that's why layoffs are less objectionable in the non-Amish setting. Yet modern business owners can still foster a familial element in their own businesses. Again, it starts from management's perceptions.

For some, it may take a paradigm shift. "It is a family," says Alvin Hershberger. "I have employees that, I'll probably cry if they ever leave me."

ON EXPECTATIONS AND BOUNDARIES

While "family" is a concept that resonates in Amish business circles, even Amish recognize that a boss can get too close. Though Alvin's employees feel comfortable enough to joke with him, he appreciates the need for limits. "They still know that there's a fine line there." Alvin realizes that "I have to watch that I don't get too personal with them, and too 'in' their lives."

Head-butting happens at times. Often when disagreements arise, Alvin says, "just to keep peace and harmony, I'll just let it go. There's times that I have to swallow it and just not say anything. . . .

"I know that I'm the boss here; I'm the one that's making more money—which I should be—and I'm the one that has more headaches," says Alvin. "So why do I want to gripe about something that's not gonna make me more money probably, and it's gonna cause me more [headaches]!"

Another experienced Amish businessperson feels "it is important to set those expectations from day one. . . . This is what we expect, and this is what we're gonna tolerate, and this is what we're not gonna tolerate."

An initiation talk can clarify expectations. Leading off with this talk helps prevent unpleasant situations later. "I never knew about that" can be preempted. The talk sets the tone for the working relationship.

Improper expectations are a common cause of employee dissatisfaction. An honest conversation about the good, bad, and the ugly of your employee's likely experience can prevent unpleasant situations occurring later.

Feedback from previous holders of the position can provide useful insight. Where did other employees encounter challenges? What has changed since then that may affect the new employee's experience?

Employees respect and trust bosses who are clear and honest about the realities of the job. And boundaries are essential to maintaining respectful relationships with employees.

FINDING A PLACE

Back at Orie Hershberger's place, we've moved from the shop to his modest residence, where the *thunk-thunk* of the blade sharpener has been replaced by the chimes of the living room wall clock.

Orie describes how he promotes a Christian atmosphere in his shop, by giving chances to those whom others might find less than ideal. One individual came to him burdened by a troubled history but with a desire to change. Orie admits that "some of the things are far from perfect, but he wants to lead a Christian life, and . . . he does what he is supposed to do."

Like some peers, Orie is not against reaching outside the cultural circle, a necessity for Amish companies needing drivers, for example. "He's not an Amish guy, he's an English guy, but . . . he sees something there that he wants," Orie explains. "He also sees that I do appreciate [him]." Another worker has a limited skill set, so Orie assigns jobs tailored to the man's abilities. Orie strives to create a welcoming, inclusive atmosphere, while at the same time running a profitable company. He knows that employees who dread coming to work are not going to be as productive as they can be, assuming they even stick around. His approach seems to be paying off. Orie's clearly pleased. You get a sense that his people are much closer to being family than faces.

ONE WALL AT A TIME

There is, of course, no such thing as a perfect employee. Fostering an atmosphere where employees can be their best requires creating a growth environment. And not just in a professional sense.

Jonas Lapp's greatest joy at work is helping his people grow. He knows that each individual has his own set of challenges. "I think everybody has a lot of talent," Jonas explains. "They just don't trust using it." Without a mentor, Jonas fears many will not realize their potential.

A good manager helps employees be the best they can be. As a mentor, this may mean helping workers deal with issues.

"It might have been a father that never praised that son," Jonas explains. "So that might be a man that needs a lot of praise. Fill his bucket, every week. For him, you look out for all the small stuff, and you make sure you compliment."

Jonas teaches his men to have "a vision." It may mean couching objectives in terms an employee can comprehend, or getting them to see tasks and challenges from a different standpoint than may be habitual.

"It might take you two weeks to put siding on a townhouse.... Well, to a guy that never had a vision, this looks like 'endless.' He never gets past the start," Jonas says. "So you teach that person that it's not about the end result today. It's about working on the day—this wall, and then that wall, and then that wall.

"To see [an employee] start making decisions on [his] own ... it's a lot of fun," Jonas remarks. "That's the best part of being a boss. It's the most rewarding part."

Employees who sense that their manager cares find it easier to trust that manager, easing communication. Ivan Miller's management philosophy involves sharing knowledge, assigning responsibility, and turning employees loose. "When I think [of] managing people, I think about helping the workers ... make the best of ... the ability that God has given them," Ivan explains.

"It never pays to manage people just so you look better. But you manage your people [so] that they can move up in life." The Amishman warns never to "keep knowledge back, 'cause that's controlling people."

Letting go can be tough. "You get it in your head you really know it better than anyone else, and you want to make sure you do it, so it gets done right. Well, if you want to manage people, you have to let them make mistakes."

When mistakes happen, "help them understand what they did wrong, and then let them go [on with the job]."

Relieving top-down pressure can improve performance. "Give them freedom to be themselves," says Ivan. "A person that's at ease with their employer doesn't make near the mistakes as somebody that's under tension all the time."

Delegation communicates that you think well enough of employees to entrust them with real responsibility. Accordingly, delegation requires holding employees accountable. But managers must know where ultimate responsibility lies.

"It's on *me*," explains furniture maker Alvin Hershberger. "I talk to the customer. I talk to the dealer. I know about it. I take it upon me to keep reminding [the employees]."

As far as his workers are concerned, "they come here to work, and they do their job, and they're concerned about getting that thing out, but they don't have to talk to the customer if it's not out. I have to."

Jonas Lapp and Ivan Miller describe the different hats a manager must wear when fostering growth among employees with diverse skill levels and personal situations. On the one hand, as Jonas explains, a manager needs to be observant enough to recognize weaknesses.

On the other hand, as Ivan demonstrates, managers need to delegate when employees are ready. Some may need less of Jonas's medicine and more of Ivan's, or vice versa. Both approaches have a place in helping employees develop. The manager's challenge is to ascertain which to apply, and in what dose. To do this effectively, first invest the time to get to know your people.

GETTING TO BUY-IN

"If you want to crush a man's spirit," says an Amishman who runs his own business while working for another, "give him meaningless work."

Seeing meaning is crucial to developing a sense of ownership. Employees buy in to a business—and feel fulfilled—when they understand the importance of what they do.

One contractor makes a point of keeping employees aware of upcoming projects. He sees their interest reflected in their questions about whether particular jobs have been secured. It reassures him that they recognize their stake in the success of the business.

A dose of transparency can help align employees' interests with those of the firm. While revealing every financial detail is a mistake, "they need to know that they're either making money or losing money," says another Amishman. Being made aware of the state of the business helps people feel more a part of its ultimate success or failure.

And when it's succeeding? Definitely *not* a time to keep quiet. One veteran homebuilder explains that while the financial incentive is important, "people love to be on a winning team." When the company is prospering, it's a lot more exciting to be around than when it's not.

The takeaway? Trumpet good news from the rafters. New customers mean the security of work in the pipeline. Plans for an innovation or change that will help the operation run better give employees confidence in a manager's ability to improve the business. Customer compliments reinforce the principle of quality work.

Keeping quiet means ignoring a powerful resource. Let your people know about—and encourage them to enjoy—positive developments in the life of your business.

Off-the-cuff and on-the-go transfers of information are a part of a business's practical functioning. But sometimes communication needs to be structured to get messages out to the organization, or to access information that only your people can provide.

OPENING THE LINES

Employees can be a great source of productive ideas and insights managers are not in a position to have. It may be a cost-save from eliminating a procedural hang-up, a smoldering fire that could be snuffed out early, or an unexploited opportunity.

But if you don't do your part to create an environment where people feel free and safe to share their ideas and opinions, you may be stifling a wellspring of knowledge and innovation.

Amishman Eli King, the son of entrepreneurial parents, has business in the blood. Eli runs a barn-building firm with his father. After observing idea exchange in the company he comanages, Eli felt something was lacking.

"A lot of times I felt like I was the only one that was coming up with ideas, and that they had the idea that mine were the only ones that were gonna roll. I don't want that."

Eli has started a regular monthly meeting. It's an improvement over the previous, more haphazard approach to employee gatherings. The set format lets Eli structure the meeting on ideas that occur to him during the month. It also allows employees to prepare their own topics.

"We've found the meetings to be very fun, because ... it brings everybody together, and it allows them to share," Eli explains. "I'm not the only one that has ideas." The meeting is meant to be inclusive and participatory. "It's open to anybody that wants to talk."

Yet bosses must remember that employees' motivations and frames of mind are often different from their own. It can take skill to coax out the information that people on the ground possess.

Elam Peachey knows some employees are uncomfortable about speaking up. "Some people are very intimidated by their employers," he points out. "The key thing would be ... if somebody does volunteer information, you don't just dismiss it.

"Even if somebody comes up ... with a suggestion that I know there is no way would work, because I've tried it, or because I just know ... it's so important not to just say 'oh, no, no, no, no; it would never work,'" Elam says. "Because the next time he won't try."

Elam suggests telling the employee, " 'I know what you mean; I saw that, and I don't think it would work, and here's *why* I don't think it would work, but I appreciate you bringing it up.' That can go a long way for the next time, having the courage to bring it up again." The "why" is crucial; understanding the rationale can make "no" easier to swallow.

Communication and Delegation

Communication runs in both directions. Managers communicate good news, expectations, and duties to employees. Employees can be great sources of ideas that improve the business. But managers must create an environment that promotes healthy communication.

In creating a functioning workplace environment, you may need to give some employees a hand. Others need to be let go. When you delegate, employees must be held accountable. But good managers know they can never delegate ultimate responsibility.

Understanding how individual efforts affect the business can help employees see meaning in what they do. But it takes communication—both formal and informal—to get key messages out to where they can have greatest impact.

Next, a look at motivation in the workplace.

TALKING DEITSCH

Among themselves, Amish speak a language known as Pennsylvania German or Pennsylvania "Dutch," a Germanic tongue sprinkled with English words.

Pennsylvania German is generally not written. Amish use English as their primary language of written communication. Books in Amish homes are typically in English. The Bible, on the other hand, is written in High German, the language of church, often with an accompanying English translation. Amish can communicate with native German speakers to varying degrees, depending on a person's dialect.

Pennsylvania German was once spoken by a number of peoples—of which the Amish were but a small part—who settled most heavily in southeastern Pennsylvania. Today, Amish and related groups such as Old Order Mennonites are among the few that still speak it as a primary tongue.

Amish children speak Pennsylvania German exclusively until going to school, where English is the primary language. Some catch on at an earlier age, particularly if exposed to English outsiders, as can be the case with children of business owners. But for most, the first big dose of the outside world's tongue comes in the one-room schoolhouse, administered by Amish teachers.

Listening to Amish converse, one can often gather a rudimentary idea of what's being discussed, due to English words appearing in the dialogue—"lawnmower" or "Belgian," for example. Amish will typically switch to English when nonspeakers are present, out of courtesy. When Amish speak English, it's often with a slight accent as well as the occasional unusually pronounced word or odd grammatical construction, such as, "It wondered me why you didn't call."

FEAR AND RESPECT

I recall my early-elementary years but vaguely. One vivid recollection stands out—of a second-grade teacher named Sister Karen and a year spent in acute terror. This was already well past the era of rulers-on-knuckles discipline, but Sister K, God bless her, sure knew how to use fear as a motivator, so much so that I dreaded coming down off the bunk bed most mornings.

At the same time, I was just about the best-behaved kid in class. At least that year. As screaming nuns, drill sergeants, and high school football coaches know, fear is a great motivator. But only on a base level. Jonas Lapp recognizes this. Instead of exploiting this raw emotion, Jonas anchors his approach in respect.

A manager who respects his employees, Jonas feels, will not say, " 'Look, I don't know how long this is gonna go this winter. . . . We got work lined up the next month, and we gotta make some money here, because we might not have work the following month.'

"That's controlling with fear," Jonas explains. "You're scaring them to work hard. That'll last . . . so long. And then the game's up."

Jonas offers an alternative to fear. He keeps his employees informed, even when things aren't going too well, but he helps them have perspective. "The better way would be to get the employees competitive *with* you." Jonas reassures his team that "if we can't compete in this, we'll find something we can compete in."

Jonas's approach gets his men wanting to do the right things for the right reasons. He realizes that fear springs from feeling limited. Jonas shows respect by leveling with employees while helping them see they're not confined to one path. It's an empathetic, feet-in-their-shoes approach.

Again, bosses need to strike a balance. Getting too close can alter employees' perception of you and may mean losing their respect. Employers must respect employees, but they also have to craft on-the-job relationships to ensure that employees do likewise. Respect should run both ways.

Ohio stoneworker Jason Glick draws the bounds in a very straight-forward manner.

"If you're out there," Jason explains, "and you feel you're taking advantage of me, I said don't look at it that way. You're taking advantage of yourself. Because we're all in this company to make money," Jason says. He points out that "if things get messed up," then "it's going to come out of your guys' pockets first, because ... the business has got to support itself."

Despite his lay-it-on-the-line manner, Jason is careful to explain his way of thinking so employees understand his motives.

"Don't think that I'm in this to get rich and retire. . . . We're all in it for that; we all want to retire someday. I said just think of it as everybody working together. It kind of works better that way."

WASHING FEET

Another way that Amish show respect is by pitching in. Employees get the message when the boss gets his hands dirty—especially when he doesn't need to. "I'll jump in and sweep the floor with them in the morning," furniture finisher Harley Stutzman offers by way of example. "Or if they're changing their filters—that's a filthy job—I'll jump in and change their filters with them."

An important principle lies behind the practice. "I would never ask an employee to do something that I wouldn't do—ever."

The idea, instinctive or learned, runs deep in the culture, and results in many owners humbling themselves for the sake of their employees and the good of their mission. And as Harley explains, even once in a while is enough. "I don't do it a lot, but I show them I care. It builds the relationship," Harley feels. "They respect me."

Another benefit is that it keeps owners tied into the work, keeps them sharp, and more aware of their employees' concerns. "I fill in as the swingman in the shop. If we have people off, I usually jump in and do that job," Harley explains. "And that keeps me hands-on," he says.

"If I never do it, I kind of lose the touch. So it keeps me on top of the game."

There are other positives in coming down off the perch. One leading Amish furniture manufacturer volunteers to work a dealer's sales floor from time to time. It enables him to see his creations from the salesperson's and customer's perspectives. It keeps him up to speed on competitors' products. And it helps him maintain conviction in his own.

The meaning of "dirty work" varies from company to company: it could be anything from cold-calling to weekend inventory to cleaning up at the end of the day. You know what your operation's least-loved tasks are. We sometimes see an idea similar in spirit to this, with bosses dishing up burgers at the company cookout, playing servant for a day. While not a job task, strictly speaking, the spirit of deference is the same, and it gets noticed. A boss can find many opportunities to show humility on the job.

Amish builder Jonas Lapp points out that when it comes to getting your employees to be effective, there's a big difference between *telling* and *showing*.

"I think a good boss won't just stand there and say, 'Hey, your piece belongs over there'; he'll say, 'I'll help you put it over there.' I think people learn faster if you help them with their part."

Pulling a person aside and showing them firsthand makes an impact, regardless of your business. For one, you are often your best trainer. Taking the time is also a nonverbal message that conveys your genuine concern.

When the boss isn't too big to do a certain task, a person is more open to what he has to say. It creates credibility. Words are weightier backed by action. And this can go a long way in aligning interests.

Unsurprisingly, the approach is similar to what Jesus' might have been. Washing employees' feet, in a sense. It may be counterintuitive, but by humbling yourself, you elevate your people. They see you in the weeds, too. They appreciate that you have your own goals, and that those goals mean so much to you that you too will take on the unpleasant tasks. And if it hasn't happened already, those goals start to become theirs as well.

PUTTING IN YOUR HUNDRED

How should a good manager react when something goes right? According to Menno Graber, "the way the Bible says.... If you want the credit, it's no good really."

Menno brings up church collections for the poor. "You know, that's like a fellow did once," Menno starts in with a wily grin. "He put a hundred-dollar bill in.

"That was a lot of money at the time," Menno continues. "So he asked the fellow, the collector, he said, 'Did you see my hundred-dollar bill in there?'

"And [the collector] says, 'Oh, I didn't know which one was *yours*.'

"So he found out he wasn't the only one," Menno chuckles. "He was the only one that said something."

Menno's quip illustrates an important point. Calling attention to an action diminishes it.

It's not enough to simply not take the credit yourself. It's about *actively* passing it on. People feel relevant when they feel they've contributed. A boss who points to himself all the time at best loses people's attention, and at worst loses people, period.

Abram Gingerich has honed his approach over three decades. "Be very willing to take the blame for whatever goes wrong," intones the Amishman, "and make sure someone else gets the credit for everything that goes right. That's a big one."

In other words, Abram says, "practice humility."

"Very few people that that comes naturally [to]," he continues. "Because we all like to feel important. And ... it's just important that we don't.

"It's important to remember that this place is going to continue ... without me. I have my role to fill here. An important part of it. But it can go on without me," the Amishman explains. "I'm just not that important.

"My prayer is always that this is not about my ego. I don't want to go there."

But "it's something which I think we all struggle with to some degree," he admits. Abram's comments dovetail with the importance his society places on community over the individual. Some things are bigger than me and my whims: God, family, neighbors, church, and in this case, a well-functioning business which serves as a vehicle for furthering the life goals of many in my community.

And in a business context it makes a lot of sense. Especially considering that many organizations suffer or fall apart when key people leave. Spreading importance, responsibility, and ability around an organization keeps priorities on the firm and holds egos in check.

One Amish builder takes a week off every year to volunteer. "When I do go for a week or so to help, where there's a disaster, I tell the men that it's because of them that I could go. That credit doesn't go to me."

Other Amish pass on good news and thank-you letters from customers. An Amish contractor calls foremen directly from the jobsite when he's on final inspection. He praises them and expresses his appreciation. The calls are a "big reward."

The net effect is that employees are encouraged to take pride in what they do. Recognition from above can be a huge motivator. Cash rewards have their place. But a word from the boss and satisfaction at knowing you did your best can have a greater long-term impact on workplace contentment, many Amish feel, than a few extra dollars.

THE POWER OF RECOGNITION

Recognition is easy to give. But it can have an outsized effect, boosting your employees' sense of worth and commitment to business vision.

Wharton management professor Sigal Barsade, coauthor of a study on the topic, notes that "one of the biggest complaints employees have is they are not sufficiently recognized by their organizations for the work that they do."

"Respect is a component of recognition," explains Barsade. "When employees don't feel that the organization respects and values them, they tend to experience higher levels of burnout."

As the professor notes, respect is an implicit element of recognition. Employees notice when a manager or boss takes the time to make accomplishments known. He's telling the organization, "I noticed, and I value you." And no one notices more than the one being praised.

Omar Zook is a big believer in the practice. "Of course everybody likes recognition," he says. "Recognition is big." And recognition is one area where seemingly little things can have game-changing impact. Some favor giving credit to the group as a whole. Others see the importance of one-to-one recognition.

"There's a lot of different ways of doing it," Omar explains. "You can stick a note in their check; you can tell them; you can tell everybody; you can tell other people to tell them." The most important thing, Omar contends, is making sure it gets out.

"Yesterday a guy called me. He said, 'By the way, you've got really good people out in the yard loading the trucks.' So now today I want to make sure I tell him that this person said what he said," says Omar. "Because I don't deserve it. He deserves it."

Effectively transmitting recognition and good news takes organization and attention to detail. But figure out a system, do it regularly, and people will start to love you for it. Work becomes more meaningful.

As a sales manager I witnessed on countless occasions the palpable impact of recognition. Time and again, salespeople would be more driven by the lure of special attention on reaching a goal. Extra money earned was often just the icing. Recognition was the cake.

To be sure, recognition is not a one-size-fits-all concept. It takes being attuned to the personality of each employee. One way of recognizing achievement may motivate a particular employee. For another it may have the opposite effect.

"You have to know the person.... I can think of employees, if I publicly would give them too much recognition, they would be miserably embarrassed," says Ohio gazebo maker Nelson Mast. "You have to kind of work with the nature of the person."

Nelson once used an employee-of-the-month program. But while some employees quietly did a solid job, they would never be publicly recognized. So he shifted to recognizing workers privately.

Nelson also points out the importance, in a larger organization, of having a person's direct supervisor deliver recognition. Frontline managers usually have closer contact with the employee than higher-ups. Recognition delivered by the top boss can make an impression. But recognition delivered by a manager who witnesses an employee's efforts every day usually comes off as more authentic and as a result can be more valuable.

Finally, the flip-side of recognition: screw-ups. They happen. How to "recognize" mistakes in the right way?

However recognition is carried out—privately or publicly—criticism should always be done behind closed doors. Embarrassing or belittling an employee in front of peers wins no love, only resentment.

Nelson Mast explains that "our company philosophy is, 'We' made a mistake. Never point out anybody individually.... We're here to correct it.

"Whoever finds out about the mistake, takes it to the person.... We don't spread it any further than we have to. But make sure the person that made the mistake knows about it."

Motivation

Respect, humility, and recognition are all important to effective motivation in the workplace. Employees respond to the servant-leader model. Leading by example, even doing the least-loved jobs from time to time, earns a manager respect.

Don't let good work go unacknowledged. Share credit and take blame. If mistakes must be corrected, always do so behind closed doors.

In recognizing achievement, well-chosen, tactfully delivered words can be worth scores.

At the same time, people are there for the paycheck. For many, financial rewards are the most important measure of achievement. So now we turn to compensation.

THE AMISH CHURCH DISTRICT

Amish life revolves around the church district. There are over seventeen hundred church districts found in over four hundred settlements across North America.

No national body exists to oversee Amish thought and theology. Individual districts hold to basic tenets. Besides the core principles universal to Amish, though, there can be much variation between individual districts and affiliations.

Amish churches are arranged geographically. In dense settlements, an entire district of roughly thirty households may fit within a half square-mile. In others, families may travel ten miles or more on Sundays for service.

When a church reaches a certain size, it will prepare to divide. The primary task is ordaining new ministry to take over the new district. Amish churches are overseen by a bishop, two to three ministers, and a deacon.

The bishop is the highest authority in the church. Ministers assist the bishop and handle preaching on Sundays. Deacons may read at service and take care of behind-the-scenes tasks such as wedding announcements and collections for members with special needs, for example.

The church ministry is highly respected. Being a part of the ministry is considered a burden and a blessing. Candidates are Amish males, usually married, and in Lancaster County especially, ideally with one or more adult children baptized in the faith. Both male and female baptized members nominate candidates for the ministry.

Receiving a threshold minimum of nominations, usually two or three, qualifies a candidate for the second round. Here the hand of God comes most dramatically into play. Nominated candidates each select a hymnal, one of which contains a verse of Scripture. He who draws the book with the verse becomes the new minister. An emotional event, fellow congregants pray for his spiritual burden to be a light one.

There is no official age requirement for the Amish ministry. In rare instances one finds ministers and even the occasional bishop in his late twenties. Typically, however, age and experience are esteemed, and ministers and bishops in particular usually show some gray in their beards.

Churches are larger in some settlements than others. In Allen County, Indiana, certain districts exceed fifty families. In some communities, such as Lancaster County, one bishop traditionally oversees two districts. Occasionally, bishops may move to a district which already has a bishop present. In the unusual settlement in Sarasota, Florida, popular among Amish retirees and vacationers, the single district lists four resident bishops.

BONUSES AND BENEFITS

"I'm there for the money," admits an Amish employee of a large Lancaster company, who also runs a side business of his own. "The other things help. Still, the bottom line is . . . I'm not doing it for fun."

The real question is how much—and when considering bonus programs, how often?

"We have fun, and I try to treat them as good as I can. And you can't do that all with the hourly pay," says Ezra Miller. Ezra prefers giving smaller periodical raises while focusing on benefits, in order to "keep the team together."

Among those benefits are summer campouts, a hit among family-oriented Amish. On rainy mornings, Ezra may treat the team to breakfast—on the clock. Ezra holds a biannual employee meeting with his accountants and IRA advisor, who offer their expertise. Ezra also says he has "an issue with a company that thinks you can't take time off of work to spend with . . . employees to teach them safety."

Company events like campouts and paid breakfast may add up to a financial expenditure equivalent to a raise or bonus. But with these kinds of extras, one thing is present that cash prizes lack: the emotional element. Sharing breakfast or being outdoors with a boss who takes the time to engage his people says "the boss cares" a lot louder than a slightly higher number on a pay stub.

Through all the extra attention, employees get the message that they matter to Ezra and the business. This may have a bit to do with his workers being with him nearly a decade on average.

EMOTIONAL EXTRAS

Cash is important, but using it as a substitute for extras and emotional involvement can be a mistake. Work environment matters as well. Do employees look forward to walking in the front door? Or given the choice, would they prefer a morning off to finally get those wisdom teeth yanked?

Ben Stoltzfus sees the issue as clear-cut. "If they like their work, that speaks louder than bonuses and money does. . . . Usually it's not the money that makes it happen.

"If you give them [extra] money, it'll work for a month or two, but it's not a long-term fix. If you know that you have an employee that's maybe thinking about quitting . . . I just don't like to go, 'Oh, I'll give you a couple bucks an hour more.'"

A simple problem remains: "They still have to come to work and do their thing! It just doesn't work in the long run," Ben reasons. "Either they like their job or they don't. And money isn't gonna make them like it."

Ben prefers helping employees enjoy what they do by creating positive workplace conditions. He believes strongly in recognition and praise. If they hate the job, extra pay is just a wasted resource. In such cases it's probably better to let that person leave.

Jason Glick is of a similar mind when it comes to nonfinancial extras. Benefits and company events may help to break up monotony. "It helps the relationships between the workers, too. If you do stuff like that together, it's not like you're just on the job, day after day after day after day."

Extras are not a given, however. Jason mentions some recent problems. Employees realize the trips and extras may disappear if issues aren't resolved.

The generous yet qualified approach to benefits seems to be bearing fruit. "It seems things run smoother at work if everybody gets along better. You know, as a friend, instead of just, 'the next employee.'"

Company events and other emotional extras can improve the bottom line. "Obviously, your jobs are much more efficient if people work together well, and get along," says Jason.

What benefits would hit home with your employees?

SHOWING THEM THE MONEY

For all the good feelings fostered by owners pitching in, for all the nice times at cookouts, and for all the kind words, "the looming reality of that mortgage payment every month pretty much dictates what you're gonna do," in the words of one Amishman. How do Amish bosses implement financial compensation, specifically raises and bonuses?

"The more hours they put in, the bigger the bonus," contractor Mose Fisher explains, describing his company's plan. "Whoever has the most hours gets a gift at Christmas."

Mose also introduces a public recognition element—passing around a list so that all employees can see rankings. Additionally, "pretty well everybody gets a raise unless [he's] not performing." The lack of a raise may serve as a subtle sign that improvement is needed. Mose's system is designed to help him keep employees as well—workers who leave the company before a set date do not participate in the bonus.

Multiple short-term financial prizes can be a bigger motivator than a single once-a-year reward. Eli King's bonus plan is time-structured. Finishing jobs within a certain time frame can earn workers extra money, usually paid within a week or two of the job's completion. His employees appreciate the fact that they have a chance to earn extra performance-based cash in the short term.

But what about quality control when your compensation system pushes speed and efficiency?

"It's actually somewhat rewarding to me that that's not the most important thing to them," Eli says. "They're not worried about that bonus as much as I thought they were going to be. . . . I like if they work towards it, but their main concern is the quality, to make sure they do it right. And to me that's worth a lot," Eli explains. "They take pride in their work."

Having employees self-compelled to do quality work is partially a function of who you choose. But an employer's example and the values she consistently promotes play a key part in building a quality culture as well.

Eli cites the value of employees taking pride at project's end in what they did. Comments from the customer or from him help them have that pride. "It doesn't take more than a few words," says Eli.

Eli's example shows that though the financial bonus element is important, balance also matters—in this case sharing the nonfinancial "reward" of positive customer comments along with the financial element of extra pay.

Eli's approach is an intuitive winner. He lets people participate in what they've created. When employees create a larger pie, they should get a thicker slice. "I feel that is our duty to share that with them." Eli offers a great example of an employer lining up employee and business interests in a forward-looking, constructive way.

THE MOST IMPORTANT COMPENSATION

Outsiders tend to perceive the Amish, with their similar clothing, names, and behavior, as a homogeneous clan. One prominent entrepreneur contradicts this idea, however, insisting that each member of the community is a distinct individual.

And as individuals—though, granted, with certain culturally specific values and goals—Amish workers pursue similar life paths and have desires analogous to other American employees: to grow on a personal and professional level, to be entrusted with responsibility, to be able to provide for a family.

The search for fulfillment in these areas is a powerful motivator. So is a feeling of belonging. A sense of belonging to a group gives the individual dignity and a feeling of worth. No one, Amish or otherwise, wants to be just another warm body.

There is value in creating a place where people want to come to work, not just to punch a clock and not motivated by fear but because of a genuine sense of camaraderie, and shared respect and accomplishment.

Those who do this well, such as Ezra Miller, Eli King, and others, are successful at aligning employee interests with their own. Their firms' prosperity and longevity attest to their effectiveness at developing a work environment conducive to employees' personal and professional success.

In the next chapter, we stay in the domain of management but shift the primary focus away from people to a related area—efficiency and productivity—with a look at how Amish managers wring big gains from small changes.

ELEVEN POINTS ON DEVELOPING AN EMPOWERED ORGANIZATION

1. Environment matters. If employees hate the job, the place, or the people, extra pay does little good. Employees are humans, not inputs.

2. *Family* is a key concept. And family can exist both at home and at work. Crafting a management approach with employees' loved ones in mind can be wise. A family atmosphere at work supports a productive environment.

3. While an authentic, engaged relationship with workers is important, so are boundaries. Maintain them.

4. Don't be shy about spreading good news. People love to win.

5. Some employees may need a bit of hand-holding. Others crave responsibility. A good manager understands which to apply. This knowledge springs from having a genuine relationship with the employee.

6. Developing an environment of communication takes effort, tact, and structure. Employees can be rich sources of business-boosting ideas. Foster an environment where they feel unthreatened and encouraged to share.

7. Getting your hands dirty earns employees' respect. Humility opens ears and minds.

8. Motivation through fear may work for a while. Respect gets longer-term results.

9. Spread credit around the organization. Recognition is powerful and can be given in many ways. How it's done depends on the employee. But always criticize in private.

10. Money matters. But so do emotional extras and benefits. People respond when they sense that higher-ups genuinely care.

11. Ideally, compensation should align employee and owner interests. Workers should be rewarded—through recognition, financially, or both—for their ideas and for improvements in the business. When employees see the success of the firm as their own, they're more apt to find solutions and contribute constructive ideas.

CHAPTER SEVEN

AROUND THE EDGES

Honing an Efficiency Mentality

Little things make a big difference at the end of the year.
—AMISH BISHOP AND BUSINESS OWNER

I pull up a seat at the end of the long table, opposite family-head Ephraim, ready for a break after three hours of barn chores.

It's been a nice stay at the Lapps', playing farmer while helping to care for the resident herd of dairy cattle. One of the first lessons guests learn in Amish homes is that you don't sleep through breakfast. Ephraim's prayer ends, and it's time to dive in.

One by one, dishes of fried eggs, thick chipped-beef gravy, and toast, butter, and jelly circle the table. I fill my bowl to the brim, and soon refill it. Shortly after, the second course arrives: cereal and hefty slabs of that Pennsylvania Dutch classic, shoofly pie.

This is usually when I reach for a fresh dish. My hosts have different ideas. Raisin Bran, Rice Krispies, and pie land right in their egg-yolky, gravy-slicked bowls. The whole mess then drowns in a waterfall of chilled milk, straight from the udder. It all ends up in the same place anyway, I tell myself, and follow the kids' lead.

Breakfast with the Lapps is an exercise in Amish efficiency. They could retrieve new eating utensils, but that would mean ten more bowls—ten more to have on hand, ten more to set and collect, ten more to wash and put away.

Ephraim's wife, Martha, has enough to do as it is. In large Amish households, little chores add up. Managing them well can mean a difference in a household's bottom line. Or extra time at day's end.

Like all meals in an Amish home, the first of the day takes place at the table, bookended by prayer—rather than on TV trays, or wolfed down on the way out the door. Amish believe there should always be time for a sit-down meal; it's not only family time but a chance to rest and recharge. Nourishment and downtime are part of taking care of the self, of maintaining the machine responsible for production.

The focus of this chapter is efficiency and productivity. Amish businesses excel in these areas, by cutting waste—through finding savings and controlling expenditures—and by making use of levers: tools, relationships, and inherent strengths.

A final component of maximizing results of time and effort spent on and in the business lies with the manager himself. A weary mind and body are more prone to error. Tending both ultimately contributes to the prosperity of the firm. Neglecting the self in an all-out push—by physically overworking, or by mentally existing inside the business twenty-four hours a day—can ruin health and damage relationships. A well-tended mind and body simply make for a more productive workday and a more effective manager.

We'll first examine ways the Amish achieve gains by finding efficiencies, and then move on to the effective use of business levers. Finally, Amish discuss issues such as stress management, acceptance, and balance, revealing what they do to keep the human machine functioning in top shape, a high-return task that must be managed like any other.

KEEPING COBWEBS OUT
OF THE CORNERS

Little brother inherits big brother's trousers. Scrap metal patches a gap in barn slats. Eggshells land in backyard pens for calcium-craving hens to peck.

An efficiency mentality dominates in Amish society, born of necessity. The demands of sustaining large families through traditionally low-paid occupations has ingrained frugal ways and cost-cutting habits into the culture.

What gets thrown out in modern homes can often be reused, hemmed up, passed down, or converted to a new function in Amish ones. Potential savings lie everywhere, from garden to barn to shop.

Business thinker Peter Drucker writes that "all businesses have access to pretty much the same resources." Drucker, however, calls *management* the sole differentiating factor between companies. "The first measurement of this crucial factor," he asserts, "is productivity, that is, the degree to which resources are utilized and their yield."

Amish business owners maximize productivity by using available resources efficiently and effectively. This means keeping an eye out for small savings of time, movement, and money.

A seemingly minor saving, spread out over time, accumulates. Getting good at spotting and eliminating inefficiencies is one way to grow a company without adding to payroll or floor space.

Ohio sawmill owner John Miller tackles efficiency from both ends. With fuel prices elevated from the 2007–8 energy shock, John switched from diesel to vegetable oil, acquired for free as a trash by-product from local restaurants. As a result, John cut fuel costs to cents per gallon, saving a thousand dollars per month—a hefty gain for his small-scale operation. Processing the oil takes extra work, says John, but the high cost of diesel justified it.

On the production end, John uses the whole tree. Leftover scrap is sold as firewood. Sawdust becomes animal bedding for area farmers. In search of more savings, John is currently studying a costlier but more durable grade of saw bands.

Another Amish entrepreneur has looked to the sun to fuel his clothes-making operation. Solar-powered devices are not accepted in all communities; however, a number of Amish do take advantage of the sun's rays to supplement power to their businesses and homes.

Roof-mounted solar cells are used to heat water, charge batteries, and power electric fences.

Ben Miller, eleven years running a furniture shop, is installing a heat-recycling device he expects will pay for itself in savings within a year. Ben tries to get his efficiency-minded approach to trickle down to his workers.

"I don't walk from point A to point B further than that," Ben explains, describing the importance of proximity. "It just makes sense to have everything closer."

"If you're doing a hundred of them, if you can save five seconds on each one, that multiplies, over the course of the year," he points out, describing savings garnered assembling wood components. "It might just be a hundred bucks, but if you want a hundred bucks, there you have it."

With more employees in the mix, small inefficiencies blow up fast. Jon Schrock can't help watching the clock when his men linger, taking a few minutes' extra break time. "Add that up over a year's time. It's amazing, if you've got seven employees." Five extra minutes tacked on to two breaks a day translates over a year to around a full week of work lost per employee.

An Ohio landscaper, whose largest expense is plants, knows the importance of monitoring material-input costs. "I've got half a dozen different nurseries where I get my stuff from.

"If you've got two to three hundred plants . . . they can vary from five to ten dollars, on one plant. It's unbelievable." Another business owner, as a ground rule, makes sure to get quotes from at least three different suppliers when purchasing materials.

Amish save on outfitting their firms as well; shops and facilities tend to be minimal in construction and furnishings. If you're running a financial institution, marble and mahogany send a signal that plywood and aluminum do not. But the typical Amish approach toward business expenditures should at least make you think twice about what a company needs in order to function—and recognize that savings wait to be uncovered in every firm, needing only the effort to find them.

SWEAT = WORK?

It may seem like common sense. But how often—with more urgent tasks calling—do managers overlook price differences, or continue to perform a task inefficiently because of a reluctance to change? And why, knowing it adds up to real money?

Some seem to fall into the "if I'm not sweating I'm not working" trap. Running numbers and scouring new product avenues may not *feel* productive. It most definitely is.

Aden Yoder gets this now.

Stephen Covey describes the dilemma Aden experienced in *The Seven Habits of Highly Effective People*. Managers' tendency is to focus on the urgent and often unimportant—the tasks that shout the loudest—at the expense of the long-term, high-impact, yet often nonurgent jobs, the ones that whisper and are easier to nudge aside.

"One of the things that I found challenging, and I should have done and didn't, was checked prices at different places more often," Aden explains, calling price differences among suppliers surprising.

"That's something that would have helped in the long run as far as money," he admits.

Aden has since sold his business yet continues to manage it, an arrangement it turns out he prefers. The current owner does pay close attention to input costs, with a staff member dedicated to monitoring pricing.

Why didn't Aden take more time himself? "I thought, well, I should be out there, *working*."

Planning and researching doesn't "feel" like work. The hard-toiling businessperson neglects it because sitting down with pen and paper seems like being lazy.

On the other hand, business advisor Isaac Smoker cautions against going too far in one direction, especially if you handle multiple roles. "You need to do pricing and planning," Isaac concedes, "but you have to know when you're doing too much of that, and not enough of actual work."

Isaac's point is to make sure that tasks actively contribute in some way to the firm. Some jobs provide the illusion of activity but achieve little of consequence.

Managers need to have a clear understanding both of their own roles and the roles of their employees—what's best handled by the manager and what should be shifted elsewhere. Evaluating, prioritizing, and allocating time require being organized.

Efficiency can save money and feed growth. "Growth doesn't necessarily mean bigger," Abram Gingerich points out. "But it could mean better, in different aspects. It could mean improving your product line."

For lunch stand owner Hannah Stoltzfus, for example, this means regularly adding new items and deleting poor sellers, while seeking to keep her offerings aligned with customer expectations of products evoking the "Dutch Country" concept.

"Growth could mean getting rid of, or selling, part of what you do," Abram Gingerich continues, "and adding something else that is more profitable, or fits better what you're already doing." Some Amish, such as interior wares seller Barbara Fisher, regularly attend product shows to stay aware of trends and acquire new goods.

Efficiency, in one sense, requires thinking through expenditures with an accountant's skepticism and being open to creative solutions.

With phones ringing off the hook and more urgent tasks calling, it's easy to push the pursuit of savings and efficiencies aside. Yet Amish owners consistently recognize the impact small gains can make—whether from an uncovered efficiency, productivity tweak, or other change—and many set aside time to pursue them. Some of those gains may be measured in mere cents. But over time, cents become dollars, and those dollars improve the bottom line.

PINCH-HITTING

White, shutterless houses. Homemade dishes from home-raised food. Bowl haircuts in the kitchen salon. In many arenas, Amish life epitomizes simplicity. But running a company is not always one of them.

While Amish—known for their faith in handshake agreements and commonsense solutions—instinctively favor the straightforward, Amish business owners have had to adapt and develop more sophisticated systems while in the thick of customer issues, production logjams, and schedule demands.

Organization makes work hours more fruitful. "Half of the work's already done," says one Amishman. "If you're disorganized and you got clutter everywhere, it just doesn't flow like it should."

Clutter can mean junk strewn about a shop, or an untidy office. In many cases, though, clutter is structural disorganization—a messy management hierarchy, with workers getting conflicting signals from different higher-ups, or with employees incentivized in counterproductive ways. Clutter often persists because of a change-averse mentality.

Alvin Hershberger leads a fairly simple existence on his back-corner Ohio homestead. But he knows that business isn't automatically simple, and that seemingly easy decisions usually take background work and attention to detail.

Alvin emphasizes organization in order to process the numerous pieces of information that come his way in a shop with multiple employees, expanding production, and a growing base of customers.

"I tire my own employees. And I tire my brother [Henry], because he's always trying to be simple. 'Just keep it simple.' I'm not. I'm like, 'Yeah, keep it simple, but don't let everything open,'" Alvin says. "I'm really into details because of that."

Alvin, who takes copious notes and relies on a Day-Timer, feels a good boss must "be multitasked" and "have a system," he explains. "You have to have a pinch-hitter."

Pinch-hitting—Alvin's term for coming through with an informed decision when it counts—is made possible when you're organized.

Setting up a system that simplifies analyzing and processing business functions, from billing to accounting to quality control, makes things that much easier.

"I'm a believer that it's the small things that count," says Alvin. "The reason a lot of people fail, is because of those small [things].... When things are really going good for you, and you're booming, you miss a lot of small things, because you don't worry about 'em.

"But when you start having to sharpen your pencil, then all at once you realize, how did I do this, without doing this?"

Lacking computer muscle, Alvin still makes sure key information flows through his business. Five copies of each order go to the five places that need to know—the boss, his brother, the manufacturing shop, the finishing shop, and the warehouse.

Alvin dutifully records details of custom jobs. Offering a year's guarantee on his furniture, he's careful to track purchase dates. Alvin's brother is his right hand in managing cash flow and billing.

"Right now, because of the way the economy is, you've got to be more efficient, and more on top of things. The small things do count." A former work acquaintance saved his employer thousands by finding a new supplier, Alvin explains. "Sometimes it's just in making that phone call."

GETTING PAID

Being organized also keeps a business's lifeblood—cash—flowing. Isaac Smoker sees a common pitfall in getting money in on time, rather than thirty, sixty, or ninety days later.

Veteran Jake Stoltzfus agrees, warning about not getting paid at all, a risk he sees as a greater threat in a tight economy. "You have to take some chances, I realize that . . . but it's gotta be smart choices," he says. "Because if you don't get paid, you're going down."

The tricky part, he maintains, is knowing when to dump delinquent accounts. Jake feels some peers follow a misguided logic which says, " 'If I cut him off, he's never gonna pay me.' "

"You better take your losses and go," says the Amishman. "The misconception is, 'The longer that I do business with this guy, the more apt he is to pay me.'" Jake's policy: "If you're behind on your bills, we don't ship to you anymore."

"In the business world, you have to trust people to a certain extent," reasons Alan Troyer, before describing a longtime customer whom he now expects to skip out on an $8,000 bill. "There's different ways to look at it. It doesn't feel good, but yeah—it happens." For many, including Alan, eight grand is not exactly horse feed. The experience has reinforced the importance of cash-flow management. Alan employs an accounting firm to send monthly statements and make reminder calls.

Alan's accountants "keep it upbeat. They don't get nasty to them or anything, they've just got to try to help them work through it . . . to keep them as a customer, and to help them out, as well as us."

Hiring an accountant "frees up my time so I don't have to do that," Alan explains. Whether you hire someone or handle it yourself, bill collection is on no one's top ten list of favorite tasks. But getting paid is a more than minor detail if the company is to stay solvent. It's just one example of how being organized can have a big impact on both the functionality and profitability of a business.

Efficiencies

Efficiency and organization are closely linked. Systematic analysis uncovers savings. Being organized makes it easier. Talking of two business-owning sons, one Amish entrepreneur sees more promise in the one who's better organized. The proof has shown itself in the purchase of a property and a growing savings account. For the second, business is "very much a struggle."

Whether you use a mental or written system, a way of processing more than one task at once is important to running a tight ship. This may mean back-burnering certain issues while taking care of higher priority ones immediately. It could mean hiring outsiders to handle certain tasks, as in the example here of bill collection.

Scour the edges for savings wherever they may be found. A buggy maker, faced with a slowdown, solicited requests from employees, who in turn offered nearly three dozen suggestions where cost cuts and efficiency improvements could be made. While "Amish business parks" of monster warehouses and production plants have arisen in places such as Lancaster County, Amish businesses are commonly situated right at home. Could yours be as well? At least early on? Are there tasks that could be subcontracted, or done remotely rather than in the office?

But be careful not to take the search for savings too far. Some things shouldn't be trimmed, especially if cuts affect quality or service in a meaningful way. Certain expenditures—seed-planting client binders used in the sales process, for example—are really essential investments in securing business or maintaining quality.

SHUNNING AND THE *ORDNUNG*

Outsiders sometimes scratch their heads at the idea of social shunning, a defining feature of Amish society. Shunning is a biblically based practice. Each Amish district observes a local *Ordnung*—a concept with roots in the ideas of "order" and "discipline"—which serves as a code of conduct of sorts, outlining boundaries for everyday life. The *Ordnung,* which describes what is permitted and what is not in terms of dress, technology, and other domains, is unwritten and varies among districts and affiliations.

Shunning is meant to help a transgressor who breaks a mutually agreed rule—perhaps by using a piece of forbidden technology and refusing to "put it away"—to see the error of his ways and return to the fold. Shunning is only applied to members of the church, not to those born in the culture but opting out of baptism into the faith.

The baptismal promise is to God above and made together with the rest of the congregation. Congregants employ shunning as a last resort after other entreaties have failed, in order to, in a sense, "shock" the transgressor into remembering and honoring his commitment.

Shunning involves social signals that indicate apartness. These can include not sharing a meal at the same table and not transacting business with the individual. Amish do not refuse aid to such individuals if they are in need. But the social barriers they erect are real and usually have a heavy impact on the person being shunned.

Shunning, say Amish, is done out of love. One Amishman who experienced shunning himself says that "most of all it is done so the soul of the deviant may be saved on the Day of Judgment."

It's also "a statement that the rest of the flock has no intention of leaving the fold and that it takes its commitment to the Lord and each other seriously."

At the same time, "shunning is usually done with great reluctance and only once there is nothing else left to do. Upon repentance," explains the Amishman, "the relationship is restored and what is in the past stays in the past."

Amish feel bound by certain Scriptural passages to employ shunning. Still, the motivation should be genuine concern for the other's soul, not moralistic self-righteousness. Says the Amishman, "the Lord is still the final judge."

LEVERS

Abe Riehl is a backcountry tomato king. His intensely cultivated organic farm spills over with a cornucopia of heirloom plants. Over forty breeds jostle for space on the Amishman's acres—Red Zebras, Boxcar Willies, Cherokee Chocolates—bursting in reds, oranges, purples, yellows, and pinks.

To run his farm, Abe relies on certain sanctioned technologies. He also innovates his own devices to help—he's created a rolling, suspended, triple-armed loader to make picking easier, for example. With the help of a few siblings and hired hands, Abe processes thousands of pounds of tomatoes weekly during picking months.

To maneuver the heavy boxes for pickup, Abe depends on another key piece of technology, a hand-operated pallet jack. Without the leverage the machine provides, Abe would be even more worn-out than he normally is at the end of a hot August day of picking.

Likewise, Amish business owners rely on various levers on a company level—tools, pieces of knowledge, or talents they use to crowbar their businesses forward.

In some cases, these levers strengthen a firm. In others, they enable its existence. Three we'll examine here are outside financing, other firms within a given industry, and personal strengths and talents.

THE MONEY LEVER

Before selling books in their communities, I was assured I'd never receive a bad check from an Amish person. This wasn't far off the mark. Some two thousand checks later, only one had ever bounced—and then only temporarily.

Amish handle money well. Finance, responsibly managed, can be a crucial lever in the growth of a business. Amish recognize the necessity of leveraging outside capital, borrowing from banks and other sources to fuel their firms. "In today's world, in a growing business, it's very difficult to be in business without being in debt," reasons a veteran. Financing allows business to happen where it otherwise couldn't.

Financial Management and Principles for Every Day Living, an advice booklet published by a veteran Amish businessperson, covers responsible finances and, especially, the power of interest—as it works both for and against an individual. In cautioning against overborrowing, the author lists half a dozen "Disadvantages of Bad Credit and Poor Stewardship," including the ideas that "People don't trust your dealings," "You'll suffer spiritual damage," and "You could suffer health problems."

Loss of trust, reputation, health, and flexibility are all potential ill effects of poor money management. The author has connected the dots to bring attention to secondary debilitating impacts of overextending oneself. Financial disaster can wreck a life—mentally, spiritually, even physically—as well as the lives of others in the fallout zone. A financial flop can harm loved ones, in addition to the families of laid-off employees, through a reduced standard of living.

Amish aren't perfect. Some occasionally land in financial straits. In such cases, Amish may employ a trustee system composed of experienced members of the community to help the debtor manage money or a business, and to nurse him back to financial health.

Such cases are uncommon, as most Amish develop a sound sense of finances, both in their one-room schools, which impart this practical knowledge to a degree, and also in everyday dealings around the home. Amish use checks nearly universally. Children handle checkbooks from a young age, shuttling them from home to barn for Dad to pay the feed salesman. Some Amish make use of credit cards as well, usually for business expenditures or convenience rather than shopping splurges.

Amish know that outside capital is a useful and often indispensable tool, but one to consider wisely. Realistic ambition, an accountant-guided review of a business plan, and honest self-examination can save future hardship.

At the same time, when using outside capital, it's important to understand what's needed. Often, the tendency is to underestimate. "Financially, we had to go a lot deeper than what I thought," says one firm owner.

"Borrow enough money so that you don't have the stress of not being able to pay the bills," says another experienced businessperson, citing the failure to put aside enough operating capital as one of the main reasons businesses fail.

"You can put everything on paper, and you probably need twice as much."

GOOD AND EVIL IN THE MARKETPLACE

When it comes to corporate mottos, Google's kindergarten-level creed—"Don't be evil"—is simple and profound. "Don't be evil" could also summarize the competitive ideal in the Amish business world, where uncodified rules of fair play and etiquette, rooted in a strong Christian orientation, check base behavior.

The Amish, unassuming and content to reside in the backstage of American society, are competitive in the business arena. Amish tacitly and explicitly admit this. One Ohio businessman, pointing out a coreligionist competitor from another state in town for a benefit sale, explained that they "lay down all competitiveness" to help make the auction happen.

Otherwise, a competitive climate exists, and the Amish entrepreneur, subject to free-market realities like any other firm owner, is forced to take this into account. While Amish businesspeople may not always like to admit it, they know that sometimes they have to do what they do better than the next guy if they want to earn more, or in some cases, even survive.

Still, Amish business owners find ways to not be evil to others in their industries. Some take it a step further, striving to be actively good—motivated by Christian altruism or by practical gains resulting from a mutually beneficial pairing. Amish-owned businesses may cooperate on multiple levels, from pooling buying power to sharing ideas to passing on surplus work when the shop is packed.

These companies have cultivated relationships. They know the same players are going to be around for a while, working in close proximity. Rather than butting heads, many Amish make themselves stronger by cooperating with their nominal rivals. And to a degree, it seems to work.

Firman Wengerd, a harness maker, is a good example of this concept in practice. Firman runs a very low-scale operation, with just a simple sign at the end of his lane drawing the attention of passersby.

Because of his reputation, Firman has been sought out over the years by others looking to learn his craft, even by those from outside his community. In a number of instances, he has unselfishly trained other harness makers who subsequently set up their own businesses, sometimes in close competition with him—two he helped set up lie within a few miles of his shop. Why?

"I keep saying I can't do it all, so why not let the other people work, too? If God gave me a chance . . . I'm here to help. I'm not here to turn anybody down." Firman, as it happens, also got a hand when he was starting.

Speaking of a local businessman he helped years ago, the Amishman says that "now he's paying me back." Firman smiles, pleased not so much because of getting what he "deserves" but rather by this example of his community working together.

"Just last week he was here . . . and he needed some material, and I needed [some] too. So we went together and bought a big bunch, for the best price."

Combining an order like this allows businesses to take advantage of bulk buying discounts. "We've been doing that for the last five, six years," says Firman, describing a practice that peers in some other industries employ as well. Firman even passes on savings and fosters goodwill by selling some material on to other harness makers at the better price. In a similar vein, thirty-year greenhouse veteran Katie Beiler describes pooling orders with competing businesses in her area to save on shipping costs.

Examples of cooperation abound within the Amish business community, from subcontracting work to companies stuck in a slow period, to alerting others to a customer passing bad checks in the neighborhood.

Instances of similar behavior show up in modern business as well. One thing visitors to Lancaster County notice while creeping along traffic-choked Route 30 are the gaudy yellow-and-purple pastel "silos" marking the local Tanger Outlet Center. Tanger, a Greensboro, North Carolina, company with locations throughout the country, was founded by shirt-industry veteran Stanley K. Tanger in the early 1980s. Tanger sought a venue to sell excess product from factory overruns and returned merchandise, and created the outlet concept in the process.

In setting up shop, Tanger sensibly sought to avoid conflict with other retailers, and thus decided to site outlets at least twenty-five miles from malls. Today, outlet shopping is a favorite pastime many associate with vacations and highway travel. Tanger's early etiquette helped to shape the direction of the entire industry, with outlets located on major interstates or near tourist destinations.

Speaking of etiquette and cooperation in his community, Jon Schrock says that "there's a lot of that in the area. . . . Even though they do almost exactly the same thing, they still work with each other, and help each other out."

However, Jon prefers *not* to share business, pointing out the problems that can occur "if something isn't done correctly." Jon fears the possibility of losing a customer's long-term loyalties. During a particularly busy time, a friend "couldn't understand why I didn't give him more work, rather than working late." Jon realized he was building a reputation and a customer base, one reason he kept his shop running twenty-four hours a day early on.

On the whole, an orientation toward mutual assistance usually overcomes any cutthroat instincts among Amish businesses. "There's enough of work around," says one Lancaster Amishman. "We're here to help each other.

"We're talking about our fellow man here. Use a little common sense," he chuckles. "Didn't you grow up with any?"

BEING GOOD IN PRACTICE: THREE GROUND RULES

With many firms concentrated in a few industries, competition happens among Amish. A few unwritten rules exist when it comes to interfirm etiquette.

Rule One: Don't Undercut

Nothing irks Amish bosses as much as competitors that cut rates excessively to capture business. Jason Glick claims he'd lost about "a year's worth of work" in the previous year due to undercutting. He says it resulted from a number of firms entering his field during flush times. The subsequent slowdown caused some to get "desperate" and cut prices drastically.

Undercutting may be the natural upshot of too many players, or it may be a tactic employed by individual firms to break into a market. Not only is it bad form, but perpetually underpricing your work is hardly sustainable in the long term. Isaac Smoker says that undervaluing work is common among newer businesspeople, "because he thinks he can do it cheaper than larger ... and older, more mature companies." Later they realize that "they're underselling themselves."

When bidding a job, Elam Peachey prefers his price to occupy the second-lowest or middle position. "The bottom guy they don't trust," he explains, "unless they got a really good impression from him." Pricing plays into a customer's perception of the company's credibility.

"No undercutting," by extension, means showing respect when vying for a contract. One contractor avoids bidding a job if he knows a neighboring business is already competing for it. Gauging a potential client, he'll contact a competitor who he knows did previous work for the person.

This prevents infringing on foreign turf but also allows him to learn of any problems with the customer, and why the other business is no longer doing work for that person. Saying it's about "integrity," he claims that in his circles, "as far as really getting competitive and getting nasty, I don't see any of that."

Rule Two: Try Not to "Borrow" Too Many Ideas

Amish are typically willing to share and likewise tap into one another's ideas. But some express mild frustration at others "borrowing" too liberally. This happens sometimes in the arena of furniture design. Understandably, some styles are standard or overlap, but creativity and innovation are respected—exhibiting a willingness to take risks.

One businessperson expressed mild irritation at a neighbor who opened up a competing shop making the same product, while admitting that "that is just part of life." For some, willingness to help expands with geographical distance. An animal-bedding producer was open to assisting a start-up in the same industry, especially since the second party was located a few counties away.

Cooperation can work. But those accepting help need to respect what the other side is willing to give.

Rule Three: Never Talk Down Competitors

You may be tempted to knock your rivals, or the work they do. Don't.

"That's one thing that's a no-no in our company—never run down a competitor's work," explains Samuel Stoltzfus. "Even though you know it wasn't right, doesn't give you the right to say it was wrong."

Samuel is adamantly against criticizing rivals "to give you a competitive edge." "Because you're not perfect either, so you're just better off being quiet, and . . . if there's any problems, fix it."

Talking a firm down often reflects more on the critic than on the criticized. For one, it usually comes off as petty and unprofessional. For another, pointing out a poor deal or criticizing a past choice never makes your prospect feel good. Praising others' work, or at least not denigrating it, shows that you honor your competitor and your customer.

FOLLOWING THE RULES

In the long term, following the rules fosters respect in the business community and ultimately results in stronger companies. A company that maintains ethical behavior, even when others don't, garners respect—both from other firms as well as from customers.

Trustworthy firms are more likely to get business and find opportunities to create synergies with other companies. One Amishman cites a company that he'd otherwise like to partner with but won't, because "they're not honest." Admittedly, when everyone else is breaking the rules, not doing so can seriously hinder a company. But in most arenas, the less ethical firms tend to be the exception rather than the standard. Over time, playing by the rules is good not only for the soul but the business as well.

LEVERAGING STRENGTHS AND TALENTS

There aren't too many Amish derivatives traders. Ditto the buggy-driving web designer. You'd also be hard-pressed to find the Old Order custom motorbike shop. Amish businesses operate within a restricted world, one delineated by culture as well as by inherent skills and ability.

Within their realm, however, Amish take full advantage of talents. Playing to individual and community strengths means getting the biggest bang for effort. Leveraging natural ability pays off; the Amish have made a mark in the building, furniture, and craft industries, establishing a culture-wide reputation in these fields.

"One mistake is thinking you can do everything," explains accountant Isaac Smoker. "And maybe you can, as far as your talent and intellect goes, but you may be better off concentrating on what you're really good at."

This works in the opposite direction as well. Weak spots help reveal a business path. Isaac is not computerized, which he admits is "archaic" in today's world. As a result, one area he can't compete in is payroll. "We can do payroll, but we'll probably charge you more than someone else will." Knowing that, Isaac concentrates on what he's competitive at.

Fence dealer Omar Zook sees discovering your own edge as part and parcel of finding a niche in the market.

"Being competitive isn't always the key for me," he explains. Omar has focused on the equine market. This allows him to use the same tools for each job, though it does entail traveling farther for work. Yet Omar feels this to be "absolutely" more efficient than dealing with the residential market.

A Plain clothes-maker has found his edge in catering to the Amish need for speed—providing off-the-rack suits for those wishing to bypass the half-year custom-order wait time. One Lancaster entrepreneur specializes in decorative wishing wells within the sizable lawn furniture market. A mother of two small children has leveraged her gregarious personality into a successful side venture selling kitchen items to others in her community.

In the modern realm, Old Spaghetti Factory founder Guss Dussin teased out a niche based on a creative approach to real estate. Dussin pursued the idea of starting restaurants in locales others considered undesirable, such as low-rent warehouse districts. The often historic buildings and unique interiors well suit the company narrative, which rests on the idea of providing a memorable dining experience that doesn't break the bank. Thanks among other things to costs kept low by an emphasis on kitchen efficiency, the chain has grown to over four dozen locations, serving over ten million diners annually.

A business direction is shaped by both inherent ability and passion. Searching for a niche may be as simple as following the classic wisdom of pursuing what you enjoy and are good at.

In business, levers abound. Amish bosses deal with cultural hindrances—restrictions against using certain technologies or legal safeguards, for example, that others would see as big obstacles. One way in which Amish businesses make up the difference is through the use of levers. The three levers mentioned here—proper use of finance, fostering productive relationships with other firms including competitors, and playing to personal and business-level strengths—are just a sampling.

Levers are waiting to be exploited. Finding them takes work, a task better performed when the manager is in top physical and mental shape. It's to that topic we turn next.

THE REAL AMISH IN THE CITY: AMISH MARKET STANDS

Across America, the city flocks to the Amish for a dose of rural relaxation. But sometimes the Amish take their show to town.

Reading Terminal Market, a stone's throw from Independence Hall in downtown Philadelphia, is a whirlwind clash of sights, smells, and sounds. Euro cheese, sushi, and shelves of African-studies texts shout for the attention of the lunch-hour hordes jostling through this century-old center of commerce.

And among the most unexpected sights in the mix are the numerous beards and bonnets working the counters.

Amish have long been uprooting themselves from the country to plant themselves for a spell in the city. Amish merchants first appeared in Reading Terminal in 1980. In the ensuing years, market stands have become increasingly popular. They're particularly common in the Lancaster community due to its close proximity to East Coast urban centers.

Markets have also sprung up in other locales. These include the Markets at Shrewsbury, located in rural York County north of Baltimore, or the Pennsylvania Dutch Farmer's Market, a short hop from the Princeton University campus.

An Amish stand owner says that in a sluggish economic climate, markets may offer a more attractive entry into business than, say, furniture making. People eat, recession or no recession. The handcrafted bedroom suite can usually wait.

There are some drawbacks, including commutes up to two hours. Days for one owner start with a 4:30 A.M. pickup and a return home as late as 10:30 in the evening.

Another drawback is the non-Plain environment. Not that Amish have anything against English people. But the market environment is admittedly more worldly than that of the farm, an arrangement which may present challenges for a people "in the world but not of the world."

TENDING THE MACHINE

Hooves are like fingernails. Or is it tires? They're described as both by the burly farriers who keep the mares, fillies, and colts of Amish America in working order. Whatever the case, horses typically need hooves taken care of every six to eight weeks, depending on the horse and the season.

Proper horseshoeing takes care and attention. Farriers develop a "bedside manner," calming jittery beasts while staying wary of flying hooves. Horseshoe removed, the hoof is filed down, after which the shoe is carefully nailed back in.

It's strenuous work, requiring the shoer to remain bent over and sweat-drenched for the better part of an hour. With manicure—or if you prefer, "tire change"—complete, the horse is ready to haul again, at least until the next scheduled maintenance.

Neglect tending the hooves, and horses can develop any number of painful and debilitating conditions. A limp appears and worsens. Soon the horse can no longer pull. Eventually, the glue factory beckons.

Just as a good Amishman maintains his horse, a manager must take pains to care for himself, to stay roadworthy and keep hauling.

Amish managers, no strangers to stress, deadlines, and challenges, maintain themselves spiritually, mentally, and physically. Neglecting one or another can mean ending up hobbled. Following are just a few examples of what Amish managers do to keep themselves out of the glue factory.

HANDLING FATIGUE AND STRESS

Planning to drop by an Amish woodshop during operating hours? Bring earplugs. The shriek of saws and pounding of air hammers put the lie to the idea that Amish life is all peace and serenity.

But it's not so much the work environment that gets to the typical Amish shop owner. "The work is the easy part," says Lancaster cabinetmaker Levi Beiler. It's things like managing cash flow and customer expectations that make business owners like Levi weary. "Sometimes there's so much stress in a business like this ... I'd just love to go out and work ... for somebody—punch the time in and go home."

"Dealing with stress itself is a job for me," says Jason Glick, while conceding that "it's just part of business." Jason seems at peace today but admits that he struggles with it. "That's what business is about. It can't be a cakewalk, if you want to be successful."

Part of managing stress is staying aware of its signs. Sometimes Jason loses patience more quickly than normal, which he sees as a warning. Another Amishman feels stress may have reached an unacceptable level "when you start to be inconsiderate to your family and people around you."

Levi Beiler acknowledges different approaches to dealing with the inevitable tension and worry. Some people rely on alcohol, he notes. "There's other ways to deal with it.

"Our best tool in that is our Christianity." Levi says that it offers "wisdom," while promoting "self-control." Weekends help too, he admits.

Alvin Hershberger agrees on the importance of faith. A minister in his district, Alvin acknowledges that "probably having issues in church, people problems . . . are harder on me than business stuff.

"If you are mentally tired, that's worse than being physically tired, because physically tired, you can go down and lay down, and go to sleep and you're better," says Alvin. "But mentally tired—it's hard to go to sleep.

"If you drink and eat right, and you keep a positive attitude, and you get eight hours of sleep, that helps a lot." Alvin, health-conscious like many Amish, takes a daily vitamin shake. A diet based around simply prepared, mostly homegrown foods can't hurt either.

Amish view stress as inevitable but also as part of the success equation. The ability to manage tension and stress level factors in when scoring how well you're doing. The bottom line: too much of it, and you're not really a success, no matter how much you earn.

"Stress is okay to a certain extent, but you need to be compensated for your stress," Elam Peachey reasons. "If you can't handle stress, don't go into business, because there's gonna be a little bit more than there is working for somebody else, unless the person's difficult to work for."

Pushing oneself to the limit may work in the short term, and may even be necessary, but it loses in the long run. Taking care of the machine means disengaging from time to time.

"You have to go on vacation; I realize that now more than I did years ago," admits Jake Stoltzfus. "You have to recharge the batteries," he explains, "and you gotta then lay it aside, for a couple weeks, or whatever it might be"—though he admits how hard it can be for someone as geared up as he is.

Besides general body-and-soul upkeep, effective stress management is rooted in proper thinking. Not being able to reach clients frustrates Elam Peachey. He's learning to accept it. "If you don't get ahold of them, that's just the way that it is.

"The end result's the same; it's just how you feel about it," Elam reasons. "If you did the best you could, the best you know how . . . you just need to let it go."

MODERATION, BALANCE, AND DOWNTIME

In Daviess County, southern Indiana, Friday night is a tough time to catch the men at home.

The reason? Dinky's.

The famous auction house in the heart of this Swiss-roots Amish community draws them in from all around. Many Amishmen, often with families in tow, make it a weekly outing, joining non-Amish from near and far to fill its 36,000 square feet, chomping burgers while bidding on shop implements, crossbows, cattle, and everything in between.

Amish across America enjoy auctions and other social occasions, some happening in large-scale settings and others, for example, local benefit events, taking place in the back lots of one-room schools. For a naturally industrious people, leisure and family time balance a life.

Amish work hard. But most realize that downtime matters. That's what Sundays are for, of course. 'No Sunday Sales' is not only an Amish business calling card, ubiquitous on signs at ends of Amish lanes, but a biblical injunction they take to heart. One day a week is set aside to honor God as well as take a load off.

There's one minor problem, though. Despite their best efforts, Amish haven't been able to convince cows on the idea of an off day. So the milking proceeds uninterrupted, though Amish dairymen refuse pickups during Sunday clock hours, forcing milk companies to send trucks late Saturday nights or in the wee hours of Monday morning.

Amish enjoy leisure time. Barefoot barnyard softball, where a cupola-clearing shot counts as a home run, is one way of spending time off. Trampolines, basketball hoops, volleyball nets, fishing poles, and pony carts afford young and old alike leisure outlets. Moderation is important, and activities accepted in one community may not be in another. Family-oriented events are typical.

Culinary delights enhance Amish gatherings. The cooking talents of Amish housewives are legend. "I enjoy eating good food," Reuben

Detweiler admits, though pointing out that "I've got to eat to live. I don't live to eat."

Prayer and spiritual activities provide perspective, capping a tough day. Daily devotions usually happen in the morning or before bed.

Devotions consist of prayer, taking turns reading chapters from the Bible, and discussing them. "Nothing fancy, but just the basics of life," explains Reuben.

As far as devotions go, Reuben says that they "get you . . . closer with God. . . . Let's say you make a habit of reading the newspaper every day. You'll think like the newspaper, right? If you read the Bible every day, you'll think like the Bible. . . . We'll never be perfect, but . . . [it's] our duty to try to do as much as we can, according to the Scriptures."

Amish know balance is important. In Amish society, there is a work element, there is a leisure element, there is the spiritual, there is family and community. They often intertwine. Helping a neighbor shuck corn or collect hay can cover two or three categories at once. Business owners may be driven, but Amish recognize that moderation prevents burnout and keeps a manager more effective and content in his life and relationships.

ACCEPTANCE

Jonas Lapp relates a tale he heard from his bishop.

A poor man owns a beautiful white horse. The horse is admired near and far. The man's neighbors wonder why he doesn't sell it and improve his material situation. Even the king would like to buy it. The man stubbornly refuses.

His neighbors call him an idiot. Then one day the horse runs away. "We told you so," the villagers say.

"All we know is what we know. The horse is gone. That's all we know," the man replies.

Later, the horse returns—with fifteen others in tow. The villagers marvel at the wisdom of the man, whose wealth has just increased exponentially. They urge him to break the new horses and sell them. "You will never have to work again."

"All we know is I have sixteen horses now," says the man.

The next day, while off riding one of the new mounts, the man's only son falls, breaking both legs. The villagers again see only a fool. Perhaps they're right? His response: "All we know is my son has two broken legs."

A week later, the kingdom erupts in war. All able young men are enlisted for battle. Many will not return. The man's son, hobbled by his injuries, escapes a likely death.

"The moral of the story is this: we only know what we know today," says Jonas. "There's nothing promised tomorrow. I have payments to make; I have a mortgage to make, on the house and the barn. I have six children to feed. If I were to run out of work, then I'd have to find something else."

Jonas puts it in God's hands. It brings him a powerful sense of peace.

With an attitude of acceptance "your life in general becomes a lot less stressful. Your body's not stressed out. You have more time. You have more joy to share with other people."

Jonas knows it's not enough to just pray and expect things to go great. He knows he has to get up Monday morning and hit it. But he's not going it alone. If this doesn't work out, something else will. His connection to a higher power gives him that confidence.

Peace of mind is rooted in acceptance, as captured in the white horse story. Becoming comfortable with the fact that much lies outside of one's own control—while doing the best to quantify and control that which you can—helps maintain both sanity and serenity.

Keeping body and mind in top shape requires active effort. Stress needs to be managed like any other element of a business. Moderation, balance, and an orientation of acceptance allow managers to stay fit and approach issues with a more serene mind. Ultimately, a happier, healthier manager is a better manager.

AROUND THE EDGES

Amish maximize the success of their firms by hunting down efficiencies, playing to strengths, and managing personal well-being. But success means more than just squeezing out the last drop of profit. In the next chapter, we examine how Amish interpret the idea of success, taking into account not only financial results but big-picture issues such as family, heritage, and the welfare of others.

ELEVEN POINTS ON EFFICIENCY

1. Where competitive fields have been flattened by information technology and widespread access to resources, productivity and efficiency gains resulting from superior management are one area where a company can find an edge.

2. Small savings add up. Take the time to find them.

3. Don't get caught in the trap that says only sweat equals work. Reserve time to figure out how to do things better. Finding efficiencies should be high on the manager's task list.

4. Real growth can come from gains in efficiency. Achieving better returns from an existing arrangement can take the place of physical or personnel expansion.

5. Being organized saves money and makes finding gains more likely. Work out a system that fits your style and covers your bases.

6. Search out areas to exploit strengths and opportunities. Potential levers are everywhere.

7. Outside money can be a powerful lever. Be realistic and measured in its use. Financial failure can land you in a hole that will take years to escape.

8. Competitors can help one another. Develop trust and team with rivals to mutual benefit.

9. Following marketplace etiquette garners respect and trust, and makes productive interfirm relationships more likely. People gravitate to those who play by the rules. Not being cutthroat means a more enjoyable, peaceful, and productive business life.

10. Play to strengths. Businesspeople who do so, do better and enjoy their businesses more.

11. Actively tend body, mind, and soul. Managing the self is part of managing a business.

CHAPTER EIGHT

THE BIG PICTURE

Getting What You Came For

I see my wife more in five years than most people do in thirty.
—AMISH BUSINESS OWNER

Slipping a bit on the slushy ice, I make my way out under the 4 A.M. February sky. Up ahead, the barn is aglow, light filling windows and seeping through cracks in the wooden doors. Church-approved gas lamps enable Ephraim to get the predawn start he needs. After all, school starts soon, and breakfast must be eaten as well. Milking, like so much else, is a family affair.

On this particular morning, Ephraim's wife, Martha, has joined him out in the barn, along with Annie, their eleven-year-old daughter. Annie alternates mornings with her nine-year-old sister Priscilla, who gets to sleep in today. The oldest children, Levi and Susanna, are old enough to be working at a neighbor's dairy up the road. Little Eli, an energetic second-grader, will join us in about an hour or so, sleepy-eyed but dead set on his tasks—tending the chickens and pigeons.

Early-morning milking is the norm. Most Amish farmers stick to a plan that has them draining *"koo* juice," as Ephraim calls it, twice a day. Farmers who milk every ten or even eight hours can achieve increased yields and higher income. However, most Amish refuse such a schedule, citing its disruptive nature and incompatibility with the rhythms of family life. "Family comes first" is Ephraim's simple answer as to why he refuses to push his herd for profit.

The family dynamic pervades Amish society. The Lapps are a classic example of an Amish farm household: independent, yet tied in various ways to other farmers in the community, and industrious, with many children who pitch in.

Home businesses have served as a substitute for the family farm, attractive in that they often offer the same dynamic—families in close proximity, working together toward shared goals.

Those goals are not taken lightly. Amish know well where they stand on issues most important to them, whether it's church, God, family, or their children's education.

Temptation exists as elsewhere, and sometimes individuals get ahead of themselves, pulled away from these core ideals. Yet Amish typically see business as a means to an end.

A thriving small business helps the family stay together, permits an owner to support fellow church members in need, and allows him to keep control over his work environment, eliminating unsavory influences and promoting the good. It generally serves these ends well.

Fledgling entrepreneurs may picture business ownership in rosy hues, only to find it just the opposite—with stress, lack of time, and financial troubles among the most common complaints.

Keeping in mind *why* you got into business can ground you and help with motivation in rough spots. In any sort of entrepreneurial activity, the *how*, the *what*, and the *when* all matter. But the *why* ought to come first.

In this chapter, we take a deeper look at the Amish *why*. Why examine the Amish *why?* Some elements of the Amish vision may hit home. But even if you don't share the same motivations as the Amish, a look at Amish drives may serve as a good launching point to review, recall, or flesh out your own reasons for being in business.

Because in the end, it's less your specific *why* that matters, and more the simple fact of having one that holds real meaning and relevance for you.

BLOWING UP

Closely connected with the question of why is a question of scale, one that arises again and again among Amish: what is the ideal size of a business?

"I've held this business back a lot harder than I let it grow," says Glen Beechy of his sprawling furniture manufacturing firm. "Every year from the first year on, I built an addition on, for the first six years."

Size is an issue many successful Amish owners struggle with, and one worth taking a look at. The modern paradigm generally tells us that bigger equals better. But is that always the case?

It's a question I've asked just about every Amish owner I've spoken with. Answers vary, with more leaning toward the smaller, more easily managed end of the spectrum. But more than a few, like Glen, have had a hard time holding themselves back.

"It's hard to know exactly when to [grow]," says Glen.

Early on, Glen found it a pretty simple equation. "If we didn't supply the customers we had, we got in trouble, so basically that told us when to grow. If we had more work than we could handle, we had to sit down and weigh our options. . . . Do we tell people that we can't build for them anymore; are we going to grow right with them?"

The decision may seem simple, but with growth adding layers of complexity and potentially introducing new challenges, it may not be obvious. Among the Amish, the small-scale ideal and close family involvement mean that bigger business is not always the clear choice. "We just kind of want to stay where we're comfortable," explains one Amish mother on the choice to limit the size of the family business, citing among other things the importance of having the family at home and working together in a close environment.

One Amish business vet warns against placing artificial numerical bounds on your firm. "What is too big? You don't say, 'Now I have thirty employees, now I'm too big.'" But pointing up the precarious balance small business owners must often maintain, he also says that more employees do not always mean more profit. "It can go the other way."

Alan Troyer, who earlier described the responsibility he felt toward mortgage-carrying employees, describes the trickiness of staying the same size while avoiding layoffs.

"You just keep looking for more work. . . . Then, if you start a new line, it really takes off, and you get behind so you can't supply the customer, then you hire more people. . . . When that slows down, then you're at the same position you were before . . . [so you] come up with a new product line. If you come up with a new line, you want it to sell, and if it sells well, you have to hire people."

Alan echoes Glen's qualms about the impetus toward growth. "It really is a vicious circle. And it's really hard to maintain a business with the same amount of employees for a long time. It's hard to be just right with enough orders. Either you're busy or you're slow."

TURNING SOUR

Jon Schrock, who has run companies in two industries, explains his take on size. "I don't want the business to grow bigger, but at the same time, if it has to, to meet our customers' demand, I guess we will."

But Jon cautions, "A business can grow too fast. If you don't have . . . a good team, and it's just going wild, and there's too many loose ends . . . then sometimes it goes the wrong way fast, too.

"It went sour," Jon explains, describing a local company that got into trouble. "The customers weren't happy with their work."

Jon cites a breakdown in customer relationships, diminished product quality, and lack of capable people as causes of this business's demise. All are common threats for any business faced with rapid growth, and ones which can prove a firm's ultimate undoing.

Another businessperson offers the example of a friend's company, at one time described by a local banker as the fastest-growing firm in the area. The Amishman calls what happened next a heads-up.

"He was really doing well. And all of a sudden . . . because of a matchbox-type building [approach] . . . adding on and not paying attention to the infrastructure ... it reaches a certain point, and it collapses."

One bad habit, particularly for nonanalytic types, is to ignore the numbers, especially when business is good. Perhaps because of a desire to economize, or to "keep things simple," they may avoid seeking the help of an accountant who could shine much-needed light.

Many feel that a more measured approach to growth—"learning to crawl before you walk, and to walk before you run," as one authority in the community puts it—is the wiser path. The experience of one interior décor business owner is fairly typical of a conservative mind-set, commonly seen among Amish, which respects the "slow-and-steady" ideal. Barbara Fisher started her business small, building it gradually over a ten-year period and avoiding the need to borrow to fund the firm. Slow and steady has paid off, as Barbara's operation eventually expanded and now enjoys robust sales at both its current locations.

Still, the prospect of quick growth can be enticing.

"It's a vicious cycle you get into," Glen Beechy explains, repeating a common perception of growth. "Unless you say 'enough,' ... we could be three, four, five times the size if I would have let it go. Back in the late '90s, we probably turned more stores down than we sold to."

That scenario would be the envy of most companies. But should the modern business owner, lacking the inherent self-restricting qualms the Amish have concerning scale and pride, really worry so much about size issues?

In other words, is this just a nice idea for the Amish, with their small-scale family aesthetic? Is it really a different story in "the real world"?

THE WRONG WAY, AND QUICK

In fact, there are plenty of examples of modern-world Icarus companies—ones who flew too high, too quick—and we know how that story ends.

One recent example comes from the modern building industry. Howard Roofing Systems was named in the late 1990s to the Inc. 500 list of fastest-growing private companies. Howard peaked at $8.5 million in revenue and a staff of 120, the largest metal roofing contractor in the country at the time. A few years later, the firm had filed for bankruptcy, as had its founder, Chuck Howard.

"We just grew like crazy and couldn't handle it," Howard explained, recounting his tale for *Inc.* magazine. "An entrepreneurial company takes on the personality of the entrepreneur. My perspective was that if we slowed down the growth, then we'd wither and die."

After a fast start and rapid growth in a virgin market, signs should have told Howard to curb expansion. Yet he pushed forward with an aggressive growth strategy, despite dissenting voices in the company. Howard was forced to take on lower-margin jobs when new, undercutting competitors entered the market. He scrambled to keep work coming in the front door in the fear that idle workers would jump ship to the competition. As money came in, there was a false sense of progress. In reality, "we weren't creating the money we thought we were," according to the company's operations chief at the time.

This resulted in a loss of $700,000 in the company's record revenue year. All the while Howard pushed for more growth, even with cash squeezed to the max. A decision to skip paying payroll taxes—freeing up funds—was the nail in the coffin for the firm. Over time, debt to the government mounted to over $650,000, a situation Howard claims he was unaware of. On learning the gory details, he knew it meant one thing: bankruptcy and the end of the ride.

Today, Howard admits that "in hindsight, the red flags should have gone up, but I was extremely busy."

Experienced builders among the Amish warn against taking on too many jobs without knowing if they will be profitable. Dennis Miller, a contractor with fourteen years of experience running his own company, is pro-growth. Yet he realizes that a steady stream of work coming in the door does not automatically mean things are going well.

"I'm always looking to grow, and I'm always looking to . . . get into new specialty markets. But your employees have to be trained . . . and it's real easy to overcommit, and then your quality starts lacking.

"My sales volume the past three, four, five years, has stayed within 10 percent. . . . It's been real steady. I'd like to increase that a little bit, but I'm very careful about how I go about doing that."

There's a reason for the caution.

"In construction you handle a lot of money. And it's real easy to get on the downside of things," Dennis explains. He points out that a miscalculation in a pricing formula may not be discovered until months later—potentially resulting in big losses.

"If I start the first of those projects on April first, it'll be September before I realize I'm losing money . . . with this pricing formula." And in the meantime, he may have signed even more contracts based on the same flawed numbers.

Dennis's example highlights why his industry is considered high-risk. Dennis has to work constantly to stay on top of details. At the same time, construction is not the only industry where caution, planning, and restraint come in handy. As some find out the hard way, being "extremely busy" can't be an excuse for ignoring the financial side.

Whether driven by greed, ambition, or adrenaline, the unchecked push for growth can be lethal. The Amish seem to realize this instinctively—or at least are reminded of it frequently by their culture.

Minister and furniture maker Alvin Hershberger, who spends his Sundays preaching to a flock that includes a high proportion of successful businesspeople, is not in it for the money.

"If I'm a millionaire, you won't notice it. If I make $50,000 a year, it's still the same. It's what I do with it, and if I share it, and I reward my employees. My goal is to let my business just grow slowly . . . but surely."

Alvin has his *why* figured out.

"My vision here is not that I'm wealthy. I don't want to be wealthy. I don't want to! Because money has hurt a lot of people," he says, acknowledging the corrupting potential of financial success.

"I'm just thankful that I can pay my bills, have a comfortable lifestyle ... [and] support missions," Alvin continues, "and at the same time be able to pay my employees, and see them being successful in their personal lives, and having something to give back to my children. . . . That's what I'm looking for," Alvin finishes, rounding out the list.

It might not sound as thrilling, but business owners like Dennis and Alvin probably sleep easier at night. They also show, by their words and example, that running a business isn't just about handling a lot of cash or riding an adrenaline wave over your competition.

FROM CHILDHOOD ...

Amish children are frequently born at home. Others come into the world in modern hospitals. Amish often prefer the nonclinical setting, relying on midwives, country doctors, or special birthing centers in their communities.

Even with a half dozen tykes already underfoot, a new baby is always a joyful occasion. Each newborn is considered a blessing. Those that come into the world "imperfect" are sources of joy—and are often teachers of lessons. When the plan is left to someone else, the children that result can only be seen as special gifts.

Amish begin teaching prime values of obedience and humility early on. Sitting at the table, I hold little Levi at six months of age, bringing his hands down and clasping mine over top. Levi sits peacefully, unresisting. Later, nearing his first birthday, the little boy has different ideas. Forcing his hands into prayer position, even for a few seconds, means bawling and rebellion. Levi's parents smile and persist, knowing it can take time to mold a child's will.

Young Amish boys often wear dresses for the first year. Diaper-changing is easier that way. This can make for humorous mix-ups, of course. By his second year, an Amish boy will dress like his father, with a hat of his own perhaps held in place by an elastic chinstrap. A little girl begins wearing a prayer covering early on, shielding from view the hair that will grow, uncut, for the rest of her life.

Home life for a child is a joyful time of imitating older brothers and sisters, chasing younger ones, and exploring the curiosities of farm, backyard, and creek. Carts and miniature ponies teach some youngsters to handle reins, while books and simple toys help pass the time in the chill of winter. Older siblings often care for younger ones, picking up skills for later in life. A six-year-old with baby brother or sister perched on one hip is not an unusual sight. Mom has peaches to can and pies to make, after all.

FAMILY TIES

An intense midsummer light streams through the windows this early Saturday morning. Delmar Wagler, a soft-spoken father of six, has picked a modest wooden toy off the top shelf of the bookcase, and is sharing a story.

The toy is a Noah's ark, and it used to be Galen's favorite, Delmar explains, as he fingers the smooth-worn surface of the wood. But Delmar's son is no longer around to play with it. It's been a few years since their boy passed on. Yet the Waglers' loss still seems fresh.

Five at the time, Galen had been waiting to cross the busy rural Indiana byway the Waglers live beside. Standing patiently as he'd been taught, he watched an oncoming car go by, then darted out for the other side. The second vehicle, which had been tailing, hidden close behind the first, hadn't a chance to stop in time.

Delmar gets quiet. His eyes have begun welling up, red.

But slowly, a smile breaks through. He knows his boy is in heaven, he says.

He just got there ahead of the rest of us.

The Amish are blessed with an abundance of children. Yet they feel the loss of one of them as acutely as any parent would. "Getting there ahead of the rest of us" is an idea that many who've lost a child express. It's a consolation that brings the focus back to the big picture. We are not here forever. A higher goal awaits.

Here on earth, children are also very important in helping Amish families function. As part of their upbringing, they are put to work—in garden, kitchen, shop, and field. Some have criticized the Amish for this practice, calling it harmful. Amish vehemently disagree.

Ben Miller, an Ohio-based woodworker, explains why having his children involved in his business is so important to him. As far as family goes, Ben says, "that's the only goal I have. I mean, obviously, we all want to get to heaven; that's the ultimate goal, but besides that, supporting my family.

"I'm not really a pessimist, but in some people's opinions I probably would be. But what more do we want?" Ben continues, "I'd like to do something [so] that I could work with my kids now. But in [the woodshop] they're going to have to wait till fourteen, and the oldest is five.

"We grew up on a farm. At five, we were milking cows. And some people would say, 'Well, it's child labor.' 'You're abusing them.' It's not abuse. It's something that every American should have done."

A business, or a farm, or even simple household tasks allow the Amish to train their children in pillar virtues: hard work, diligence, obedience, trust in God. In this sense, the home business plays a key role, contributing to what the Amish seek to accomplish by living within close-tied Christian communities.

SHE'S THE BOSS?

In business, children play a role, and so do spouses. Family involvement means that instead of a business taking parents away from the home, it can bring them together. The degree of involvement may vary, but Amish recognize the importance of this dynamic. Vernon Troyer, who finishes furniture in Ohio, explains some good advice he once received.

"My wife ... she helped a lot with it. . . . My business wouldn't be where it is, if it wouldn't be for my wife. I'm serious," he says, citing counsel given him early on by a veteran entrepreneur.

" 'Let your wife take care of all the billing, all the paperwork. . . . If she's got questions, help her.' But he said get her involved. The more you get her involved, the more successful you're gonna be. And it's worked," Vernon explains, obviously satisfied. "The only time I get upset is if there's no money in the checkbook!" he chuckles.

Vernon theorizes on why the husband-wife dynamic is so important.

"You're more together." The Amishman pauses, then reaches for an example from modern America. "You know, a lot of the English, I'm not, you know, saying anything bad, but let's say your wife, she goes out here to work today, you work somewhere else—you barely see each other. And that's where a lot of divorces are coming in."

Vernon points out, though, that it's not just non-Amish who have work-related marital issues.

"I'm not knocking on anybody.... We've got problems—some Amish ... well, one of them thinks one way, and the other one thinks the other way; they can't quite agree ... and the first thing you know, they need counseling," Vernon explains, "and it's just for the simple reason that they do not work together."

Some female Amish firm owners may involve their husbands in the business by partnering with them or with husbands playing an assisting role. At the same time, the majority of businesses are managed by Amish men. Wives often take on a prominent part, and not just in getting their men to poke their heads in the door more often. They also aid in decision-making, contributing raw labor, offering input on hiring, and so on.

Christian King credits his wife for much of the success of his business, calling her "a backbone."

Having a business at home has advantages and disadvantages, Christian explains. His wife has the flexibility to be there for the children before and after school, to help Christian in the shop, and to coordinate the kids' involvement. She fills in when time is tight and orders are due, putting in occasional predawn hours.

He and his wife will always discuss new ventures, Christian says. He listens to her opinion when considering things like loans and expansion. Above all, he counsels preserving harmony, starting on the domestic front.

"If you're gonna be unhappy at home, you're gonna be unhappy at work too. That's just the way it is. Whatever's inside your heart's gonna come out."

BALANCING ACT

The little ones have their say, too. Samuel Stoltzfus knows when he's been working too hard. When his little girl starts telling him not to go in the morning, he gets the point.

Ohio sawmill owner Orie Hershberger offers a nugget of wisdom, plain yet profound. "There are not too many things that are automatic. You gotta control things." It takes conscious effort to prevent slipping into bad habits and neglecting the important things. Balancing family and work is just one of those things.

Amish are known for their industriousness. Crack-of-dawn milkings, barn raisings, and a society centered on manual labor all attest to that. But can simple hard work ever get to be too much? Even the Amish can overdo it, skewing too far in the direction of work while leaving insufficient time for family.

Omar Zook offers simple pointers he's internalized over his twenty-one years in business, as we sit in his office on a chilly February morning. "Quit at a certain time. Go home to your family.... It can wait till tomorrow. You don't have to finish something today.

"Sometimes it's good just to be away from it."

Omar's sprawling business is located about fifty yards in front of his modest family home in rural Pennsylvania. Fifty yards is close—sometimes *too* close. Omar feels the proximity is both a blessing and a challenge.

It's easier to stay connected to work; but as he found out, sometimes that's not a good thing. For a while, Omar was staying out too long, too often. Customers would come by at odd hours. He felt obliged to be out to take care of them. At some point, he knew he had to make a change.

"My wife helped me with that. She controlled that pretty much. I'm so happy about that. I would be the type to stay out till eight o'clock at night. And I was really glad for her to help me with that," Omar explains. "We started that probably about six years ago," Omar says. "It works really good. ... I'd rather turn it off, and leave it off. [I'm not]

living here—I'm living in there!" says Omar, nodding in the direction
of home.

SUCCESS STORIES

The stock numbers of business—sales, profits, income—tell an objective
tale of achievement. But sometimes success can be subjective. One man's
paradise can be another's fallout zone. Definitions of success vary among
Amish as well.

"Personally, success is peace in my heart," explains Jonas Lapp.
"That's number one. In business, I think it's to have peace in your
business.

"And through that, it's like a well-oiled machine. You don't have
people back-biting.

"Some of my brothers are like, 'Yeah, but you gotta have a vision,
you know; you gotta make goals, and at the end of the year—'

"And I say, time is measured in years by man. By God, it's just
every day. Every minute."

Success starts with knowing yourself, says Ben Miller.

"Each person has to have an idea of what he wants to do in life,
and that will reflect what he does with his business.

"I'm more concerned with my personal life, and I'm just using my
business to support my family, and [to be] able to work at home."

Ben admits that this approach has not meant tremendous growth.
"We've stayed close [to] the same in sales, and in profits, for the last,
probably eight, years. Maybe I'm falling back, I don't know."

While Ben recognizes the importance of keeping "new ideas on the
table," the lure of a huge business does not drive him.

"I have no desire to have forty employees, and a billion dollars."
Ben chuckles. "That's not what I'm after. . . . We could die tomorrow."
When asked if some people lose track of the big picture, Ben replies,
"Absolutely. Money takes over, in my opinion. And that's not good. . . .
Let's not get into that."

As for his own situation, "Yeah, I make some extra cash," Ben admits. "I don't starve. But I don't make a ton of money."

HANDING OVER THE REINS

While some might not, others definitely *do* make what could be called "a ton of money." Though it may not be immediately obvious on an Amish Country drive-through—judging by the appearance of homes and clothing—there is a lot of cash flowing around many business-oriented Amish communities today. In *Amish Enterprise,* Donald Kraybill and Steven Nolt point to numerous local sources who attest to this success. One in-the-know financial officer cited in the book states plainly that "the huge wealth created by Amish businesses in recent years is simply staggering."

But racking up big bucks tends to lose out in importance to other measures of prosperity among the Amish. As discussed earlier, a business can also be considered a success if it serves as a vehicle for achieving core goals.

Each Amish individual has a personal conception of what constitutes doing well. At the same time, generalities emerge, such as being able to be a provider to the community as well as supporting a large family. Other common notions of success are rooted in concepts such as heritage, mentorship, and transition.

For many it's about transferring a functioning entity, one which those who follow actually *want* to take on, a tool that perpetuates a lifestyle and values that its owner holds dear.

Like other Amish businesspeople, Abram Gingerich shares the desire to have a business that provides a living and a place for his children to work.

"And then to be able to pass this on, and keep it going to the next generation, so that it can continue to do that. My goal is not to build something . . . of great value, and then sell it."

Abram is mulling the impending transfer of control to his sons, currently working under him in the business. The changeover is already underway. For Abram, it's a new challenge in a long career filled with them.

"I sense that this is part of the transition to the next generation, and the hard part is accepting the fact that we're now there. It was always me that was running the show, and doing everything, and all of a sudden, I see myself starting to fade out of the picture, and it's not necessarily a good feeling."

But Abram knows that in the end, having people you've groomed and trained to take the reins, and who are capable and willing, is perhaps the best reflection on a business owner's legacy one could hope to have.

... TO OLD AGE

Time comes to hang up the hat. But among Amish, that means anything but tee times and bingo nights. Even after ostensibly retiring, many Amish remain quite active into old age. With work in the blood, it's hard to just kick back and do nothing.

On retiring, Amish grandparents traditionally move into what is known as the *dawdihaus,* a smaller structure often built onto the main house. Living in close proximity to a child's family allows grandmothers to help care for grandchildren or tend to kitchen and garden while grandfathers lend a hand in the fields or shop. The aged and experienced are esteemed and their wisdom valued.

Grandparenthood means lots of grandchildren and great-grandchildren, sometimes numbering in the hundreds. Old age in Amish society means never having to be alone. Nursing homes are rare final destinations for Amish, and most grow old as an integrated part of the community.

Amish do not participate in government-sponsored retirement programs, having negotiated an exemption from the Social Security system, neither paying in nor receiving payouts. The community steps in if they need help. Amish retain dignity as they move into the twilight of life. The aged are neither forgotten nor brushed aside.

GIVING BACK

Business owners, as job providers, mentors, and generators of wealth, are well-positioned to positively affect lives. To many, the chance to give back is a prime source of satisfaction and a role they take on readily. *Giving back* makes up a big part of the vision of numerous Amish.

"My challenge is ... I get some boys that have difficulties at home with their parents," says Ezra Miller, explaining a task he relishes. "I love that.

"I don't like [that] it happens," he clarifies. "But I love them boys." Ezra takes them on board and puts them to work.

"That's a challenge for me. To show them that there's a group of people around, that enjoy what they do, with respect. It won't go long until they'll have respect for their parents."

Though necessity dictates they not run rehab centers under the guise of businesses, some Amish are receptive to the idea of taking on employees that others may see as damaged goods, in the best cases manifesting a Christlike compassion for human shortcomings.

This may mean giving second and sometimes third chances to employees who screw up, especially if they see that that person has struggled or had a harder time of it than others.

The marginalized and downtrodden in wider society get attention as well. While experiences vary, some cite contributing time and money to missions as among the important extracurricular activities they engage in. Numerous Amish, businesspeople and nonbusinesspeople alike, donate their time and skills in rebuilding projects and disaster cleanups in both Amish and non-Amish communities.

When Amish businesspeople reach a certain level of achievement, they may take on advisory and mentoring roles, fostering a positive business environment for others. A number of the larger, more successful business owners in this book give back by participating in business organizations and advising other businesspeople.

Others become mentors within their own businesses. Jonas Lapp makes sure to remind his employees that "this company might be just a stepping-stone for them to better themselves."

I'm a bit surprised to hear that, even though I know Jonas to be concerned with his people's well-being. Even so, it seems that encouraging your employees to go somewhere else—creating competition out of your best people, in whom you've invested a lot—could be a nice way to drop a hammer on your foot. Is he sure?

"Oh, absolutely. . . . We won't be here long! . . . I'm not building a company to be here forever. 'Cause when I leave, it's gone."

GETTING BACK?

Are Christians destined for better things by virtue of their faith? Do true believers get a leg up in the earthly scheme of things as well?

While it's unlikely that any Amish person would claim to make faith deals with the Man upstairs, many do acknowledge the psychic benefits that come from strong religious conviction. Others are convinced of divine intervention—not the lightning-bolt-from-the-heavens type but more a helping hand that comes your way when you do the right thing consistently.

Alvin Hershberger sees obvious benefits in being a practicing Christian. Perhaps faith in a better life to come enables us to do better in this world, he supposes.

"You actually have an edge over the world. . . . You know this is only for a time. This is only for a season. You know that you have got something better coming," he says. "So you think that I want to live that, and I want to share that with other people—look what kind of effect that can have.

"And if you really stop and think about it, it's a win-win situation. Because people can sense that; they know that," Alvin says. "And when they know that you're true at heart, that makes a difference."

One misinterpretation would be to construe this to mean that a person would do well to go out and "get faith" in order to get more customers.

"We talk about God in our newsletters," one Amish wholesaler explains, "but we don't believe in just putting it in for a sales promotion."

At the same time, it's prudent to put down another misinterpretation: that nonspiritual people cannot do well at business. Plenty of modern examples prove that false.

Yet you can't ignore the benefit the Amish get from their reputation, and their actions, which reinforce it. It obviously brings personal contentment as well.

Amish are unlikely to see it through this prism. Alvin, for instance, chooses to do good for the sake of it. He knows it brings him benefits—abundant relationships.

"When I die, what is gonna be the number one thing that people are gonna say about me?" Alvin asks. "That he had a lot of money? I hope not. I hope that's the last thing they say about me. He had friends. He believed in God, and he had friends. That's the main thing I want people to say about me.

"Because to me, having a business, it doesn't matter if you've got three hundred workers or fifty workers or ten workers. It's the effect that you make on people in life."

REVISITING A VISION

I'm out with Ivan Miller, my wholesaler friend, once again. A thresher churns a field behind us, slowly making its way up and down the rows of Ohio corn. Ivan is taking some time off from his company today and helping bring in the crops at a relative's. He's taking a moment to share his big picture as we sit in the late September sun.

"If somebody would come and ask us to buy our business . . . it's really not for sale," Ivan explains. "A lot of people say, 'Well, anything's for sale if you give enough money,' but we have so many people that depend on us for their income, it's more than just making money; we feel it's a service to the community.

"And I like people too good. I don't know what else I'd like better than what I'm doing. . . . I love it. There's barely ever a day I don't feel like going out to work. There's down days, but that doesn't mean we have to be all out of sorts."

In contrast to the predominant view among the Amish, Ivan comes off sounding quite pro-growth. "We're growing, and we don't really have intentions to quit growing at this point. I realize some people would disagree with that. But personally, in our type of business, if you decided to just simply quit growing, you're gonna go backward.

"Now if you have a little family woodworking business, and you have a few customers, you're happy with that, that's fine. In distribution, the margin is tight. You gotta move a lot of volume. It's just the way it is.

"And the people . . . that are trying to stick to the idea of milking fifteen cows, not employing anybody or just staying really small—you have to have a certain amount of profit or you cannot pay your bills. There's medical, dentist, and all that kind of stuff. . . . It's unrealistic to think about staying very, very small. It's tough."

Ivan brings up a dilemma some Amish owners face regarding size. In his opinion, some approach the matter in the wrong way.

"I feel too many people, they have in their head they're going to stay a very small business. Well, that very thought is not very competitive," Ivan points out.

"Now, we Amish try to think we're not competitive, but if you want to stay in business, you've got to be competitive!

"Now just because you're . . . competitive doesn't mean you're not humble," he explains, getting back to a prime tenet of Amish belief. Thinking about it, I suppose to myself that pride is actually a choice that a person makes on reaching success. Prideful people have learned and chosen to have that approach to life, just as the humble have maintained a different sort of outlook.

Ivan wants to make sure I don't misunderstand. "I don't promote big business. But what some people call big business isn't what others call big business," he elaborates. "Once you're able to totally monopolize on everybody else, that's big business."

In Ivan's view, negative emotions like greed and jealousy are beasts that can strike anyone, anywhere, no matter if you sport Gucci and gold or suspenders and a chin-beard. "Human nature's universal," he emphasizes.

"I like to see other people make money off of me. I really do," he explains. "I don't like to cut all the middlemen out. To me, it's whatever it takes to get that thing out on the market. I mean, you've got to keep the price within range, but if the guy below me makes more money than I do, and I'm making a good living, why should I be jealous of him?

"He's still ... promoting my thing! To me, it's very important not to worry if somebody else is making a lot of money, even off of you. It's more important to ... try to make a nice living and be thankful for what you have, and be thankful for other people's successes," he explains. "If you're not, you're not going to have a success yourself."

THE BIG PICTURE

Gratitude. Family focus. Looking out for the other guy. When it comes to business, the Amish haven't reinvented the wheel. One thing Amish excel at is applying certain time-honored principles—hard work, treating people fairly, providing quality goods and services—consistently.

Long-term business success entails formulating a big-picture vision, a guiding *why*, and following through on it in the day-to-day. Your vision may include many, or few, of the values and goals laid out here. That's of less importance. The crucial part is knowing what it is, for yourself.

Of all the things a manager or business owner must know, this self-knowledge is perhaps most important. From the *why* springs drive and ambition. The *why* checks a person who is in danger of overstepping limits or sacrificing integrity. And fulfilling the *why* is what brings real joy and contentment in the long run.

TEN POINTS ON THE BIG PICTURE

1. You can't take it with you. Will others want what you leave behind? That question can be a good starting point.
2. Definitions of success may vary. Yours will differ from others'. Determining it takes examining personal values.
3. Bigger is not necessarily better.

4. Business is never static. Opportunities to grow will present themselves. Expect some growth, but have a plan to manage it.

5. Success is not just measured by money. It's also measured by how well you stuck to your core goals and the positive impact you had on others.

6. Figure out what is on and off the bargaining table for you, personally. If family time is the number one thing, you may need to be careful how much you take on. Or get family involved. Understand what you're willing to compromise on before you start.

7. Your business is not necessarily a zero-sum game. Markets expand, and the success of new products creates demand for related products and services— demand that others may fill. It's okay if the other guys make money, too.

8. Life balance is important. And it takes active management to maintain.

9. Taking the focus off yourself and sacrificing for others, through charities and mentoring roles, for example, can be one of the most rewarding elements of a business experience.

10. Becoming the richest, biggest, or most powerful may not necessarily be the best reason to open a company. Hopefully, it's about more than just ego.

CONCLUSION
Barn Raising

E zra Miller used to be obsessed with his business.

Not anymore.

Ezra's wake-up call came when his mother passed away, some years into running his building firm. That's when he knew it was time to "drop the tools," as he puts it. "We're not here to stay."

Now, "I don't go evenings," Ezra says. "I'm a home person."

Ezra knows he has to tend his company. But he realizes he can't forget the more important parts of life. Family before business is how priorities stack up now.

In reconnecting with his big picture, Ezra also realized the importance of his relationships with his employees. Ezra began to delegate more and entrust his men with more responsibility. Superhero business-people exist in myth alone. And especially in a growing business, those who try to do it all on their own usually finish quickly.

No one can survive solo. The community-oriented Amish recognize this, perhaps more than most. Relationships—with employees, customers, mentors, other businesses—are crucial to the success of their firms.

And as we've examined, a big part of creating a successful company is tending those relationships. Trust, integrity, and honesty, formed and fortified over years, cement the bonds Amish bosses enjoy.

The Amish may seem different when sighted through binoculars. Hopefully, the voices in these pages have helped dispel the idea of Amish as alien. Though they may exist in a separate socioreligious sphere—"in" the world, but not "of" it—the Amish are a part of American society: real people, with dreams, flaws, and concerns just like the rest of us.

The lessons of Amish business are simple. Simple does not mean easy, of course. In applying the lessons, begin with one or two ideas that appeal to you. That may mean seeking out a mentor, taking a deeper interest in your employees' lives, or inviting feedback from customers in order to see the business through outside eyes.

Amish agriculture revolves around the barn. It's where animals shelter, equipment is stored, and feed is kept. The barn fulfills a practical function, but in the big picture it's something more. The barn is the linchpin to the operation's success and, by extension, to a contented life. Before business, barns were integral to all Amish lives; they continue to be so for many today.

But sometimes barns burn down.

A barn takes a long time to build if it's just you and a hammer. Invite a hundred helpers over, and you can put one up in a day.

You may find yourself facing a pile of smoldering ashes, or just in need of an overhaul. But whether you're starting your barn from scratch, or looking to pound a final few pegs, it's worth asking: who's helping *you* raise *yours?*

RESEARCH AND
INTERVIEW METHODOLOGY

Formal recorded interviews were conducted over the period from September 2007 to February 2009, primarily in the two largest Amish communities, that of Holmes County and contiguous counties in Ohio, and Lancaster/Chester Counties in Pennsylvania. These two communities were selected because of their high number and diversity of Amish-owned firms as well as longstanding entrepreneurial culture.

Individual businesses were selected to reflect variety in terms of size, longevity, and industry. In total, sixty business owners were formally interviewed. Businesses break down as follows (some operate multiple companies or could be classified in multiple categories; in such cases, only the business from which they derive the majority of income is listed):

A. Business classifications
Furniture/furniture related: 19 (32%)
Construction/remodeling/construction related: 11 (18%)
Leather goods/harness shop: 5 (8%)
Gazebos/fencing/outdoor structures: 5 (8%)
Sawmill/outdoor wood related: 5 (8%)

Metal/machinery/welding: 3 (5%)
Accounting/bookkeeping: 2 (3%)
Foods/market stands: 2 (3%)
Clothing: 2 (3%)
Buggies/horse-drawn equipment: 2 (3%)
Horseshoeing: 1 (2%)
Bicycles: 1 (2%)
Painting: 1 (2%)
Landscaping: 1 (2%)
TOTAL: 60

Interviews lasted up to two hours. Certain owners were interviewed multiple times. Businesses range from zero employees to thirty-eight employees in one instance. The largest have sales turnover exceeding $1 million, and sometimes greatly exceeding that figure. Though some part-time businesses were included, most represented the primary source of income for the interviewee.

Reflecting roles typical of Amish society, the large majority of interviewees were men, though some women participate in or run their own firms—typically crafts, quilting, or food-related businesses. Some interviewees were Amish women, and in addition to author interviews, information was used from transcripts of interviews with female entrepreneurs conducted by Florence Horning, as part of ongoing research into Amish entrepreneurship supported by a grant from the Ewing Marion Kauffman Foundation.

B. Businesses ranked by size: number of employees
0–4 employees and/or primarily family: 35 (58%)
5–9: 10 (17%)
10–14: 5 (8%)
15–24: 6 (10%)
25 and above: 4 (7%)
TOTAL: 60

C. Businesses ranked by longevity: current owner's tenure

0–4 years: 11 (18%)

5–9: 15 (25%)

10–14: 20 (33%)

15–24: 10 (17%)

25 or more: 4 (7%)

TOTAL: 60

BIBLIOGRAPHY

Allen County Indiana Amish Directory. 2005.

"Amish Quick to Rebuild Area Hit by Tornado." *Associated Press*, November 25, 2005.

Belkin, Lisa. "A Doctor for the Future." *New York Times*, November 6, 2005.

Brown, Paul B. "Attitude Isn't Everything, but It's Close." *New York Times*, August 6, 2006.

Buller, Burton. *The Amish: Backroads to Heaven.* DVD. Massanutten, VA: Buller Films, 2007.

Burke, Daniel. "Self-help or Scam?" *Lancaster New Era*, October 13, 2005.

Church Directory of the Lancaster County Amish. Gordonville, PA: The Diary, 2002.

Covey, Stephen. *The Seven Habits of Highly Effective People.* New York: Free Press, 2004.

Drucker, Peter F. *The Essential Drucker.* New York: HarperCollins, 2001.

Eicher, Willis, and Barbara Ann, comps. *Daviess-Martin County Directory: Directory of the Old Order Amish.* Loogootee, IN: Prairie Creek Printing, 2004.

Einstein, Mara. *Brands of Faith: Marketing Religion in a Commercial Age.* New York: Routledge, 2007.

Feldman, Amy. "The Trap." *Inc. Magazine*, January 2007.

Findeis, Jill L., and Stephen M. Smith. "The Rapid Rise of Amish Micro-enterprises." *Rural Development Views* (Pennsylvania State University) 2(2) Fall 1994.

Gerber, Michael. *The E-Myth Revisited: Why Most Small Businesses Don't Work and What to Do About It*. 2nd ed. New York: HarperCollins, 2001.

Godin, Seth. *All Marketers Are Liars: The Power of Telling Authentic Stories in a Low-Trust World*. New York: Portfolio, 2005.

Hill, Sam, and Glenn Rifkin. *Radical Marketing*. New York: HarperPerennial, 2000.

Hostetler, John A. *Amish Society* (4th ed.). Baltimore: Johns Hopkins University Press, 1993.

Igou, Brad, comp. *The Amish in Their Own Words*. Scottsdale, PA: Herald Press, 1999.

International Directory of Company Histories. Farmington Hills, MI: St. James Press.

Johnson-Weiner, Karen M. *Train Up a Child: Old Order Amish and Mennonite Schools*. Baltimore: Johns Hopkins University Press, 2007.

Kraybill, Donald B. *The Riddle of Amish Culture* (2nd ed.). Baltimore: Johns Hopkins University Press, 2001.

Kraybill, Donald B., and Marc A. Olshan, eds. *The Amish Struggle with Modernity*. Hanover, NH: University Press of New England, 1994.

Kraybill, Donald B., and Steven M. Nolt. *Amish Enterprise: From Plows to Profits*. (2nd ed.). Baltimore: Johns Hopkins University Press, 2004.

Lapp, John K., Jr. *The Social Booklet: Principles for Everyday Living*. Self-published. New Holland, PA, 2008.

Miller, Jerry E., comp. *Indiana Amish Directory: Elkhart, LaGrange, and Noble Counties*. Middlebury, IN, 2002.

"More than Job Demands or Personality, Lack of Organizational Respect Fuels Employee Burnout." India Knowledge@Wharton, November 15, 2006.

Nolt, Steven M. *A History of the Amish* (2nd ed.). Intercourse, PA: Good Books, 2003.

Nolt, Steven M. "Who Are the Real Amish? Rethinking Diversity and Identity among a Separate People." *Mennonite Quarterly Review*, July 2008: 377–394.

Raber, Ben J., comp. *The New American Almanac 2008*. Gordonville, PA: Gordonville Print Shop, 2008.

Stevick, Richard. *Growing Up Amish: The Teenage Years*. Baltimore: Johns Hopkins University Press, 2007.

Strauss, Steven D. *The Small Business Bible*. Hoboken, NJ: Wiley, 2008.

2008 Lancaster County Business Directory. Kinzers, PA: DavCo Advertising, 2008.

Umble, Diane Zimmerman, and David L. Weaver-Zercher. *The Amish and the Media*. Baltimore: Johns Hopkins University Press, 2008.

Welles, Edward O. "Why Every Company Needs a Story." *Inc. Magazine*, May 1996.

Wengerd, Marvin, comp. *Ohio Amish Directory: Holmes County and Vicinity*. Walnut Creek, OH: Carlisle Press, 2005.

ACKNOWLEDGMENTS

I'd first like to thank the dozens of Amish business owners who contributed to this book, for their patience and generous offer of time and insights. Their participation made this book possible. Amish friends offered meals, companionship, and a place to lay my head on many occasions, for which I'm grateful. I'm particularly indebted to the half-dozen Amish friends and acquaintances who read the manuscript at various stages and offered helpful critiques. This book is better for their assistance.

I'd like especially to thank Donald Kraybill, who encouraged me to pursue this project and who offered insightful advice and critiques throughout. *Amish Enterprise: From Plows to Profits,* cowritten with Steven Nolt, helped inspire the idea for this book.

I gratefully acknowledge the support of the Ewing Marion Kauffman Foundation for this project. I was similarly fortunate to have Lucille Snowden's support, through her endowment of the Snowden Fellowship at the Young Center for Anabaptist and Pietist Studies at Elizabethtown College.

Young Center Director Jeff Bach offered much-appreciated ideas, encouragement, and use of Center facilities. Jeff and others at the Young

Center, including Stephen Scott, Cynthia Nolt, and Hillary Daecher, helped create an ideal venue for research and writing. Hedda Durn-baugh and Elaine Mercer cheerfully arranged and accompanied me on a fruitful visit to Amish businesses during the research phase.

I extend a special thanks to Mark Biernat, James Cates, Alek-sandra Gosciej, Karen Johnson-Weiner, Leonard Nelson, and Patrick Vaughan, as well as Chris Adams, Henry Bedford, and Dan Moore at the Southwestern Company, for their readings, ideas, and encouragement on the project—often dating to its earliest stages.

Amish rely on mentors to learn the ropes of business, and Kevin Johnson, Thomas McDow, Richard Reeve, and Chris Samuels were among the mentors who contributed in key ways to my own early business education, for which I am also grateful.

I was fortunate to have the wise guidance of my agent, Giles Anderson, in helping this project see light. And I especially appreciate the enthusiasm and vision of senior editor Karen Murphy, as well as the diligent and professional assistance of her colleagues at Jossey-Bass. They have all helped to make this a stronger and more polished book.

Finally, I'd like to thank my family for their patience over three years' work and many long absences in Amish land. I am blessed to have their understanding, love, and support.

E rik Wesner is an Amish researcher who served as the 2008 Snowden Fellow at the Young Center for Anabaptist and Pietist Studies at Elizabethtown College, where he studied Amish business success. He worked for a decade in management and sales at the Southwestern Company, a 150-year-old publisher and bookseller, where he set an international company sales record. Erik runs marathons, speaks Polish fluently, and writes "Amish America," a popular Amish-theme blog, at amishamerica.com.

INDEX

A

Acceptance, 179–180

Accountants: bill collection by, 163; seeking advice from, 14, 43, 148, 167

Advertising: of "Amish miracle heater," 63–64; as element of marketing, 59–62; word of mouth as, 87

Advice: from outside sources, 43–44; reluctance to ask for, 18–19; from spouses, 192–193

American Marketing Association, 50

Amish: diversity among, 17–18, 151; marketing using label of, 53, 58–59, 63–64; media stereotypes of, 3

Amish business owners: number of, ix; relevance of experience of, 3, 205–206; self-care by, 175–180; women as, 12–13, 193

Amish businesses: financial success of, ix, x–xi, 2; productive relationships with other, 167–172; running, vs. working for employer, 8–10; types of, 10–11, 207–208; in urban areas, 174–175. *See also* Starting a business

Amish church: baptism into, 40; district organization of, 147–148; services of, 34–35; shunning members of, 164–165

Amish culture: vs. Amish religion, 53; conversion into, 40–41; people leaving, 34, 41–42; restrictions of, as obstacle to doing business, x, xvi

Amish Enterprise (Kraybill and Nolt), 196

NOTE: Names of Amish people are fictitious. See author's note on page xix.

consideration for family of, 130–131; delegating responsibility to, 105–108, 135, 139; expectations of, 133; as family, 129–130, 132; fostering personal growth in, 134–136; giving second chances to, 146, 198; handling problems with, 119–122; importance of, to success, 127–128; laying off/firing, 123, 131–132; motivating, 140–147; summaries of points on, 124–125, 152–153; work atmosphere for, 128–129, 133–134. *See also* Hiring employees

The E-Myth Revisited (Gerber), 8–9

Erickson, Gary, 24

Ethical behavior, and competition, 167–172

Ewing Marion Kauffman Foundation, 208

Expectations: of customers, 85–86; of employees, 133

F

Faith: as aid to stress management, 176–177; benefits of, 199–200; as grounding Amish business owners, 5; presence of, in Amish businesses, 21–23

Family: balance between work and, 178–179, 183–184, 194–195, 205; consideration for, of employees, 130–131; elderly members of,

197; employees as, 129–130, 132. *See also* Children; Women

Farming, 1, 10, 51

Fear: neutralized by focus, 6–7; as problem for start-ups, 4–5

Financial management, 166–167

Financial Management and Principles for Every Day Living, 166

Fisher, Barbara, 160, 187

Fisher, Mose, 113–114, 122, 150

Frito-Lay, 14

Frolic, 103–104

G

Genetic conditions, 117

Gerber, Michael, 8–9

Getting smart. *See* Education

Gingerich, Abram, 37, 47, 60–61, 79, 96, 143–144, 160, 196–197

Glick, Jason, 84, 112–113, 123, 141, 149–150, 170

God, ever presence of, 21–23

Godin, Seth, 52, 62

Golden Rule, applied to customer relationship, 82–83

Graber, Menno, 75–76, 82–83, 119–120, 143

Growth: big-picture view of, 185–190, 200–202; borrowing money for, 166, 167; fostering, in employees, 134–136; by hiring employees, 109–110; self-limiting, 16–17

H

Hard times: community spirit to overcome, 31–32; as learning opportunity, 18–21

Helprin, Mark, 14

Hershberger, Alvin, 45–46, 49–50, 51, 53–55, 81, 130–131, 132–133, 136, 161–162, 177, 189–190, 199, 200

Hershberger, Orie, 128–129, 133–134, 194

Hewlett-Packard, 14

Hiring employees: for attitude, 113–115; character as qualification when, 116–117; to expand business, 109–110; to fit into work atmosphere, 133–134; observing nonverbal signals when, 112–113; from other companies, 108; summary of points on, 124–125; "template" approach to, 111

Holmes County, OH: names in, 108, 109; as research site, xv, 207; tourism in, 86

Horning, Florence, 208

Howard, Chuck, 188

Howard Roofing Systems, 188

I

Igou, Brad, 117

Intercourse, PA, 84–85

It's Not About Me (Lucado), 46

J

Johnson-Weiner, Karen, 33

K

King, Christian, 89, 193

King, Daniel, 19–20

King, Eli, 38–39, 67, 68, 69, 89–90, 137–138, 150–151

Knepp, Abe, 31, 32

Knowledge: acquired in working for others, 29–30, 31; gained from hard times, 19–21; needed to start a business, 7–10, 18–19; obtaining, from outside counselors, 8, 43–44; offered at McGrane Institute seminars, 41–42. *See also* Education; Learning

Kraybill, Donald, 196

L

Lancaster County, PA: Amish farms in, 1; business seminars in, 41–42, 44; construction boom in, 30; interrelatedness of Amish in, 117; names in, 108; as research site, xv, 207; tourism in, 59, 84–85, 86–87

Language, 34, 139

Lapp, Ephraim, 155, 183–184

Lapp, Jonas, 3–5, 6, 15, 97, 111–112, 131, 134–135, 136, 140, 142, 179–180, 195, 198–199

Lapp, Martha, 156

Lapp, Sadie, 12–13, 88